Empowering the Faculty
Mentoring Redirected and Renewed

by Gaye Luna and Deborah L. Cullen

ASHE-ERIC Higher Education Report 3, 1995

Prepared by

Clearinghouse on Higher Education
The George Washington University

In cooperation with

Association for the Study
of Higher Education

Published by

Graduate School of Education and Human Development
The George Washington University

Jonathan D. Fife, Series Editor

Cite as
Luna, Gaye, and Deborah L. Cullen. 1995. *Empowering the Faculty: Mentoring Redirected and Renewed.* ASHE-ERIC Higher Education Report No. 3. Washington, D.C.: The George Washington University, Graduate School of Education and Human Development.

Library of Congress Catalog Card Number 96-77447
ISSN 0884-0040
ISBN 1-878380-68-0

Managing Editor: Lynne J. Scott
Manuscript Editor: Barbara Fishel, Editech
Cover Design by Michael David Brown, Rockville, Maryland

The ERIC Clearinghouse on Higher Education invites individuals to submit proposals for writing monographs for the *ASHE-ERIC Higher Education Report* series. Proposals must include:
1. A detailed manuscript proposal of not more than five pages.
2. A chapter-by-chapter outline.
3. A 75-word summary to be used by several review committees for the initial screening and rating of each proposal.
4. A vita and a writing sample.

ERIC Clearinghouse on Higher Education
Graduate School of Education and Human Development
The George Washington University
One Dupont Circle, Suite 630
Washington, DC 20036-1183

This publication was prepared partially with funding from the Office of Education Research and Improvement, U.S. Department of Education, under contract no. ED RR-93-002008. The opinions expressed in this report do not necessarily reflect the positions or policies of OERI or the Department.

EXECUTIVE SUMMARY

The concept of quality improvement has been incorporated into higher education within the last decade. Incumbent with this concept is the empowerment of college and university faculty—to harness their talents and skills and promote their professional growth. For years, business and industry has applied the philosophy and principles of mentoring to attract, retain, and promote junior employees, and mentoring has improved individual and corporate performance and effectiveness.

In translating these same concepts of mentoring to higher education, strategies, guidelines, and programs have been developed and implemented to empower faculty through mentoring. For example, mentoring has been known to invigorate senior faculty, to help junior professors learn the ropes, and to assist female and minority faculty members in understanding organizational culture.

Mentoring embraces a philosophy about people and how important they are to educational institutions. *Empowering the Faculty* synthesizes the literature on mentoring in terms of conceptual frameworks, mentoring arenas, and roles and functions of mentors and protégés. It also discusses the dynamics of mentoring for empowering faculty members as leaders and the importance of mentoring women and minorities in academe. A discussion of planning mentoring and faculty mentoring models focuses on developing and empowering faculty to ultimately benefit the institution.

Why Should Academe Be Concerned with Mentoring?

Not only does mentoring develop the profession; "by not mentoring, we are wasting talent. We educate, and train, but don't nurture" (Wright and Wright 1987, p. 207). The literature overwhelmingly points to benefits to the organization, the mentor, and the protégé. Mentoring is useful and powerful in understanding and advancing organizational culture, providing access to informal and formal networks of communication, and offering professional stimulation to both junior and senior faculty. Mentoring is a continuation of one's development as defined by life cycle and human development theorists in terms of life sequences or stages, personality development, and the concept and value of care (Erikson 1963; Levinson et al. 1978).

How Does Mentoring Empower the Faculty?

Mentoring supports professional growth and renewal, which in turn empowers faculty as individuals and colleagues (Boice 1992). Teaching and research improve when junior faculty are paired with mentors, job satisfaction and organizational socialization greater. Not only do protégés become empowered through the assistance of a mentor, but mentors themselves also feel renewed through the sharing of power and the advocacy of collegiality.

Can Mentoring Assist in Faculty Leadership?

Experts in the field of mentoring point out that mentoring is developmental and continuous, and may address a variety of faculty career needs over a period of time. Faculty can develop as leaders through the receipt of professional and institutional information; support, sponsorship, and stimulation; advice, assistance, and guidance; and feedback and direction toward goals. Faculty involved in mentoring are more likely to have opportunities to develop not only professionally (career orientation) but also personally (psychosocial needs) over the span of their careers (Kram 1986).

Does Mentoring Involve Special Considerations?

Research emphasizes the benefits of mentoring programs and the successes of those who have experienced mentoring. But mentoring must fit the culture and environment of the educational institution, and faculty must be involved in the design and implementation of strategies and plans for mentoring. Mentoring might need to address the concerns and needs of women and minorities in academe. Statistics and research studies point to these professionals' experiences in higher education as different in terms of scholarship, advising assignments, teaching loads, and service to the community, profession, and institution. As a first step, mentoring has been important in assisting new female and minority faculty members to feel comfortable with the academic environment (Maack and Passet 1994).

What Can Institutions Do?

Empowering the faculty through mentoring requires careful planning so that the educational institution's needs are incorporated. Although mentoring programs have similar steps, purposes, and activities, programs need to be customized to meet the goals of the protégés, the mentors, and the community college or university. Recommendations include raising campus awareness about the importance of mentoring, establishing a mentoring program with faculty assistance and input, providing recognition to those who participate, and providing support through institutional resources. Planned mentoring programs include establishing purpose and goals, assessing the organization's policies, identifying and training participants (both protégés and mentors), and evaluating and modifying the program.

What Must Be Done in the Future?

Although informal mentoring programs are often found in community colleges and universities, no existing body of literature synopsizes or analyzes these programs. What works well at one educational institution is not readily known to others interested in developing mentoring programs. Planned, formalized mentoring programs are even rarer, and some of those that exist have failed to determine evaluative outcomes in terms of protégés, mentors, and institutional goals and objectives. Those interested in mentoring research need to identify those programs that have been successful and understand why. And research on the specific benefits of mentoring programs for female and minority faculty members—at both the community college and university levels—needs to be conducted.

CONTENTS

FOREWORD

College faculty spend many years in formal education learning the content of the subject matter of their chosen academic area, but they have very little formal training in the knowledge, skills, and procedures necessary to be successful in their profession. Most often, the first teaching style used by new faculty members is the teaching style they found most successful for their own learning. By modeling the skills of a favorite professor, they hope to become the favorite teacher to their students. A major weakness in this process is that there is little or no communication, few observations, and minimal follow-up, if any, between the faculty member and the role model.

The training and nurturing of faculty in other significant skill areas, such as publishing, designing examinations, assessing students, participating in faculty governance, or establishing a research agenda, receives even less formal training. Even lower on the list are discussions and critical examinations of basic values in ethical areas like the validation of student assessments, defining standards for faculty performance, and the ethics of research.

Increasingly, the concept of faculty mentoring is seen as one process that can be used to overcome these gaps in the education of a faculty member. While it seems logical that a junior faculty member could benefit by working with a senior and more experienced faculty member, it is now being recognized that a mentoring relationship also has great value to the senior faculty member. Mentoring relationships that are established to achieve specific objectives, such as developing new teaching techniques, making presentations at national meetings, or developing a research agenda, assist both parties in developing a greater awareness of both their profession and their role in the profession. A formal mentoring relationship legitimizes the examination of the knowledge and skills needed to accomplish specific objectives, and a successful mentoring relationship establishes higher self-esteem and a greater sense of appreciation for both parties.

This report by Gaye Luna, professor of educational leadership at Northern Arizona University, and Deborah L. Cullen, professor and director of the respiratory therapy program at Indiana University School of Medicine, carefully examines the mentoring process. The authors insightfully discuss the empowering nature of mentoring and then, after examining the experiences of non–higher education organizations with the mentoring process, they look at some of the basic learning and developmental theories that underlie the mentoring framework. The authors give considerable attention to the benefits of mentoring in promoting the success of minority and women faculty members and conclude with an examination of several models of mentoring programs.

In the long run, an active mentoring program will have as many benefits to the institution as it does to the individuals involved. Foremost among these "mentoring advantages" is that trust between faculty is enhanced; additionally, an intellectual synergy is created, a greater sense of purpose is developed, and basic faculty issues are more easily resolved. This report forms a comprehensive knowledge base for faculty and institutions that want to establish a mentoring program or assess their current mentoring activity.

Jonathan D. Fife
Series Editor,
Professor of Higher Education Administration and
Director, ERIC Clearinghouse on Higher Education

ACKNOWLEDGMENTS

The authors wish to convey their love to their children, Erik Grant Luna and Megan Katherine Cullen Loescher. Although recognized as educators, administrators, scholars, and community and academic professionals, the authors' greatest roles are as mothers. Their lives have been enriched because of these two very special young people.

INTRODUCTION

Educational institutions have restructured work settings to incorporate the concepts of quality improvement. This restructuring has included everyone from managers who want to increase organizational productivity and reduce costs to academic department chairs who want to increase faculty members' effectiveness to presidents who are looking for new ways to meet the challenges of the economy and to respond to uncertainties.

Educational organizations realize that the improvement of quality involves empowerment and that empowerment harnesses the talents of individuals within academe, promotes those individuals' professional growth, and provides benefits to the organization. Mentoring, whether practiced informally or formally, advances the concept of individual and institutional empowerment by supporting employees' growth. For decades, corporations have applied the philosophy and principles of mentoring to promote junior employees, to improve individuals' and groups' performance and effectiveness, to plan for the succession of leadership, and to increase company morale. These same benefits of mentoring can be applied to higher education and empowerment of the faculty.

The first section, "Mentoring and Empowerment," provides a general history and background of mentoring and a synopsis of mentoring in the field of education. With private sector mentoring providing the foundation for mentoring in higher education, the second section focuses on corporate mentoring, differences between mentoring in business/industry and academic settings, and the benefits of mentoring in the workplace. The next section, "Mentoring Frameworks," discusses primary mentoring frameworks and theories and the comparison of mentoring concepts and functions. It is followed by a discussion of mentoring and faculty development. The next two sections offer specific information on the mentoring of female and minority faculty members. "The Application of Mentoring" discusses recommendations, guidelines, qualifications for mentors and protégés, and models of mentoring. The final chapter provides conclusions and recommendations.

Mentoring, whether practiced informally or formally, advances the concept of individual and institutional empowerment by supporting employees' growth.

MENTORING AND EMPOWERMENT

Education is experiencing economic, social, cultural, and political challenges, and community colleges, colleges, and universities today are not immune from the questions and demands posed by consumers, taxpayers, and governing bodies. The general challenge can be characterized as the expectation for quality postsecondary and higher education with fewer dollars and other limited resources. In academe, empowerment is fundamental to quality improvement in terms of productivity and effectiveness, and mentoring within an institution provides an avenue to empowering educators. Mentoring promotes faculty productivity, advocates collegiality, and encourages a broader goal of attracting, retaining, and advancing faculty members. Mentoring supports professional growth and renewal, which in turn empowers faculty as individuals and colleagues (see the section titled "Mentoring and Faculty Development").

Various institutions have successfully used the concept of mentoring. In education, the value of mentoring faculty members and forming mentoring relationships is correlative to those benefits found in other work environments.

Educational programs can increase understanding of mentoring and its role in career development and create a learning context in which relationship skills and positive attitudes toward mentoring can be developed. In addition to enhancing knowledge, skills, and attitudes, effective education can change the culture of an organization by reinforcing new values that give priority to relationship-building activities (Kram 1986, p. 186).

Traditions of Mentoring

Mentoring has existed through the years in a variety of forms and settings. Although mentoring has been defined differently in the fields of psychology, human development, human resource management, and education, the overriding purpose of mentoring has been the professional and/or personal development of an individual—the protégé (protégée) or mentee.

One historical definition of mentoring comes from the mythologic story, *The Odyssey,* by the Greek poet Homer. Homer profiled the faithful and wise "Mentor" who was entrusted to nurture and protect the King's son in the absence of his father. In this literary description, "Mentor" was immortalized as the guide and counselor who groomed the young prince for leadership. Similar images can be found in more recent popular characterizations—Shazam in Captain Marvel comics, Yoda in *Star Wars,* and Zazu in *The Lion King,* for example. Other notable illustrations of mentoring include the fraternal associations of Socrates and Plato, Freud and Jung, and Haydn and Beethoven.

The popularity of the concept of mentoring was introduced in the educational arena through the research of Levinson, Darrow, Klein, Levinson, and McKee (1978), whose longitudinal study pointed to the importance of mentoring relationships in young men's adulthood. Mentoring defined in terms of the character of the relationship and the functions it serves includes several responsibilities:

- *A teacher,* by enhancing an individual's skills and intellectual development;
- *A sponsor,* by using influence to facilitate an individual's entry and advancement;
- *A host and guide,* by welcoming the individual into a new occupational and social world and acquainting the individual with its values, customs, resources, and role players;
- *An exemplar,* by providing role modeling behavior (Levinson et al. 1978).

The most crucial function of mentoring a protégé was to "support and facilitate the realization of the Dream . . . believing in him, sharing the youthful Dream and giving it his blessing, helping to define the newly emerging self . . . and creating a place in which the young man can work on the Dream" (Levinson et al. 1978, pp. 98–99).

Through his psychosocial theory of the formation of lifespan personality, Erikson (1963) posited a stage of generativity that included the concept of mentoring. Erikson defined the natural, age-sequenced evolutionary state of generativity as including the concern for making a better world for the next generation. This stage encompassed conditions beyond the individual's own development and immediate family and focused on a generative life mentoring younger adults. This natural stage in an academic environment provides a twofold purpose: developing others and promoting the organization.

Whether mentoring is reviewed from a protégé's or a mentor's point of view, the concept of mentoring has been expressed as a history of relationships, relationships that have fostered individual growth. These relationships may be long term, structured, formal, or planned. Or they may be spontaneous, short lived, or informal. In all of the traditional examples, the relationships have surrounded a basic foundation of human and organizational survival: sharing skills, culture, beliefs, and values. The origins of mentoring and foundational work that followed at a much later date have provided an organizing framework for research on the mentoring process.

Academic Mentoring

The majority of literature describes mentoring as the relationship between a senior member of an organization and a junior colleague wherein the senior employee takes an active role in the career development of the younger professional. Mentoring in higher education has been defined as follows:

- *Mentoring is a process by which persons of superior rank, special achievements, and prestige instruct, counsel, guide, and facilitate the intellectual and/or career development of persons identified as protégés* (Blackwell 1989, p. 9).
- Mentoring in education is the socialization of faculty members learning the rules of academe (Carter 1982).
- *[Mentoring] involves a special kind of socialization for leadership roles. . . . The process is one of extending and expanding personal efficacy and influence* (Moore 1982, p. 28).
- Mentoring involves colleagues who are role models, consultants/advisers, and sponsors for peers (Schmidt and Wolfe 1980).

Mentoring has additionally been defined as part of the efforts to explain the complexity of work and occupations as categorized in the *Dictionary of Occupational Titles* (DOT), a data source that delineates the nature of occupational work in the U.S. economy (U.S. Dept. of Labor 1991). An analysis of classifications in the dictionary compares educators' work with work performed in other occupations

(Rowan 1994). One of the worker-function scales includes mentoring, which the dictionary defines as "dealing with individuals in terms of their total personality in order to advise, counsel, and/or guide them with regard to problems that may be resolved by legal, scientific, clinical, spiritual, and/or other professional principles" (U.S. Dept. of Labor 1991, p. 1005).

If education is viewed as a transformational journey, then mentors can be seen as guides and mentoring as processes of modeling, maintaining tradition, offering a map, conceptualizing, and providing a mirror (Daloz 1986). With regard to faculty members as mentors to students:

> *Few teachers or mentors ever see a student through an entire journey. Rather, we accompany students along some legs of some of their journeys, and if we are to play our part well, we need to view their movement with a broader eye, to see whence they have come and whither they are headed* (Daloz 1986, p. 42).

Although a widely accepted operational definition of academic mentoring has yet to be determined, the focus of mentoring remains on the growth and development of a protégé. Indeed, the diversity of definitions allows higher education institutions the freedom to discuss mentoring in terms of empowering faculty members.

Mentoring and the Culture of Higher Education

Higher education possesses its own culture, one defined as a total system with distinct structural features, role relations, informal system dynamics, and environmental stresses and strains (Ballantine 1989, p. 428). The maintenance and promotion of a set of values can be found in this system, and for higher education to preserve its culture, new members must be oriented and initiated into the institution's system. As well as sustaining the culture, mentoring assists professionals in their academic and professional development. Educational institutions that have successful mentoring programs (see the appendix) have shown that universities and colleges do look for innovative ways to empower faculty members.

As research has revealed, the mentoring process "can contribute significantly to the dynamic development of [the] profession. . . . By not mentoring, we are wasting talent. We educate and train, but don't nurture. We should be concerned with capitalizing on the young professional's talent" (Wright and Wright 1987, p. 207). Moreover, academics have pointed out that the inspiration and guidance of a good mentor is "a given . . . one of the nearly indispensable ingredients of a successful career" (*Chronicle* 1992, p. A7).

MENTORING IN THE PRIVATE SECTOR

Mentoring is used in the private sector as a tool, strategy, or technique for the development of employees. Junior employees are often empowered through mentoring relationships, learning not only about their jobs but also about the "shadow organization"— defined as "an all-too-real parallel entity based on power and politics that is only faintly reflected" in a company's documentation (Zey 1984, p. 1). Moreover, organizational literature points to a strong link between mentoring and the career advancement of these junior employees.

Private sector mentoring can be translated to academic settings. The translation in practice in some cases is uneasy; however, the guiding principle of mentoring, to assist in the development of an individual, remains the same, whether the environment is academic or business.

Corporate Mentoring

The terminology for the mentoring relationship varies in business and industry. The term "sponsorship" is used to explain the interaction between junior and senior colleagues (Dalton, Thompson, and Price 1977), whereas "networking" (Michael 1992) and "role modeling" (Hanson 1983) characterize mentoring in other studies. Moreover, mentoring can be distinguished in terms of traditional mentors, supportive bosses, organizational sponsors, professional mentors, patrons, and invisible godparents (Phillips-Jones 1982). This comparison of mentors reveals the varying conceptualizations of mentor types and mentoring functions in the corporate world:

1. *Traditional mentors* are defined as older authority figures who protect, advocate for, and nurture their protégés over a long period of time.
2. Persons in direct supervisory roles are *supportive bosses.* They perform the same functions as traditional mentors but serve more as coaches on a regular basis.
3. *Organizational sponsors* are mentors at the top whose major function is to assist in the promotion of the protégé.
4. Combining a variety of functions involving career counseling and advising, *professional mentors* are paid for their services.
5. *Patrons* use their financial resources and status to help protégés prepare for and launch their careers; often such mentors are relatives and friends.

6. *Invisible godparents* are mentors who help protégés reach career goals without their knowing it (Phillips-Jones 1982).

Definitions

Definitions of mentoring from the field of management and organizational behavior include a "relationship between a young adult and an older, more experienced adult who helps the younger individual learn to navigate in the adult world and the world of work. A mentor supports, guides, and counsels the young adult as he or she accomplishes this important task" (Kram 1985, p. 2). A mentor is "someone in a position of power who looks out for you, or gives you advice, or brings your accomplishments to the attention of other people who have power in the company" (Fagenson 1989, p. 312). And a mentor is a senior professional "who shares values, provides emotional support, career counseling, information and advice, [and] professional and organization sponsorship, and facilitates access to key organizational and professional networks" (Olian, Carroll, Giannantonia, and Feren 1988, p. 16).

Categories

Additionally, the culture of business organizations can determine the titles and roles of mentoring. Terminology for organizational mentoring has been categorized according to sponsor, role model, and mentor as shown in table 1 (Murray 1991, pp. 11–13). Mentoring is further defined in terms of facilitated mentoring, "a structure and series of processes designed to create effective mentoring relationships, guide the desired behavior change of those involved, and evaluate the results for the protégés, the mentors, and the organization" (p. 5).

Private sector research

Some of the first studies on mentoring were conducted in the 1970s in the private sector (see, e.g., Collins and Scott 1979; Dalton, Thompson, and Price 1977; Kanter 1977; Roche 1979). Researchers studied primarily male professional work populations and used retrospective interviews in their research. Findings focused on the mentored stages in a professional career and the verification that successful business-people have had at least one mentor. One model with successive stages of career development delineated mentoring functions required of each stage (Dalton, Thompson, and Price 1977; see also Kram and Isabella 1985). Roche's research on mentors (1979) created additional attention when his findings pointed out that professionals with mentors earned more money at younger ages, were better educated, were more likely to follow career plans, were happier with their careers, and derived greater pleasure from their work (see also Short and Seeger 1984). Hennig and Jardim (1977) found that fatherlike sponsors were a necessity for women to reach top management positions in their corporations. Phillips (1977) noted similar results in her study of 331 female managers and executives; however, she cautiously concluded that while mentors play a critical role in career development, "it is too early to say without question that all women [and men] need career mentors" (p. 123).

Business and industry have used mentoring to address corporate needs, including planning for succession, developing leaders, linking career management systems to career-planning systems, promoting diversity in the workforce, meeting the requirements of affirmative action, and reengineering the company. Research has pointed out the numerous benefits of mentoring for private sector organizations, and "[mentoring] is simply the best method of passing along the norms, values, assumptions, and myths that are central to an organization's successful survival" (Wilson and Elman 1990, p. 93).

Different Environments

The development of leaders in educational organizations has been considered less important than in business and industry (McNeer 1983). This assumption provided the foundation for McNeer's research on differences in mentoring between the two environments. Careers in business and industry have often been sustained within a single corporation, which allows for continuing, close relationships through the career of a protégé (although this situation may be changing). Careers in educational administration, however, are more mobile and mentoring relationships more varied and short lived. Mentoring could be the solution to social, business, and economic problems, including companies' pursuit of innovation, the prevalence of industry consolidations, the need for diversity in the workforce, shortages of labor, and

". . . [mentoring] is simply the best method of passing along the norms, values, assumptions, and myths that are central to an organization's successful survival."

TABLE 1
MENTORING IN BUSINESS AND INDUSTRY

SPONSOR

An active booster or advocate of any number of people within a company. A sponsor is constrained by only time and generosity. The sponsoring relationship is informal, with neither person making any commitments of responsibility or interaction.

Activities of a sponsor:
- Making introductions to top people in the organization;
- Making introductions to others with influence in the industry or profession;
- Making recommendations for advancement;
- Reflecting power on the sponsored person by publicly praising accomplishments and abilities;
- Facilitating entry into meetings and activities usually attended by high-level people;
- Serving as a confidant;
- Offering guidance in the customs of the organization.

ROLE MODELS

Role models can perform the same activities as a sponsor or can simply be held in high regard by any number of people without even knowing that they are viewed in this favorable light. There is no particular structure to the role-modeling relationship. It can continue as long as the observer sees positive behaviors to emulate.

Role models often exhibit:
- Success and exemplary behavior in achievement and style;
- An ability to get things done;

the evolution of global corporations (Zey 1986). Mentoring can enhance an industry's emphasis on total quality management and quality assurance (Caldwell and Carter 1993).

The literature on mentoring in business and industry has compared mentoring and career stages or cycles (see, e.g., Burack 1984; Dalton, Thompson, and Price 1977; Josefowitz 1982). Although the career stages or cycles are classified differently in numerous studies, the assumption is that protégés move through a continuum, with mentoring assistance available throughout the various levels. Such career-mentored stages are not as prevalent in education. Moreover, mentoring as a fast-track method of identifying and developing management talent can be found in recent business studies, but the concept of a "fast track" is rarely used

- Knowledge of organizational policy and philosophy;
- Apparent enjoyment of position and accomplishment.

MENTORS

Typically, there is one mentor to one protégé, and each knows what is expected of the other. The mentor carries out some or even all of the functions of the sponsor and role model in a relationship structured around the development of skills.

Mentors perform one or more of the following functions:
- Act as a source of information on the mission and goals of the organization;
- Provide insight into the organization's philosophy of human resource development;
- Tutor specific skills, effective behavior, and how to function in the organization;
- Give feedback on observed performances;
- Coach activities that will add to experience and skill development;
- Serve as a confidant in times of personal crises and problems;
- Assist the protégé in plotting a career path;
- Meet with the protégé at agreed time intervals for feedback and planning;
- Agree to a *no-fault* conclusion of the mentoring relationship when (for any reason) the time is right;
- Maintain the integrity of the relationship between the protégé and the natural boss.

Source: Murray 1991, pp. 11–13. Reproduced by permission.

in educational literature. And corporate mentoring models do not always fit the complexity of an academic environment, where a number of key relationships exist. A requirement exists in education, different from business and industry, that "faculty interact on different levels within the campus community . . . and because [of] both the job market and the channels for disseminating research . . . it is important to create a [mentoring] model that presents an array of relationships going beyond the day-to-day interactions" (Maack and Passet 1994, p. 16).

A dearth of information exists regarding evaluative outcomes for mentoring faculty, and the mentoring research in postsecondary and higher education has revolved primarily around whether mentoring relationships have existed for protégés, either as students or as professionals, and what benefits have been accumulated.

A study of 235 associate and full professors of education regarding their mentoring experiences as students indicates that those who were mentored were more likely to mentor others (Busch 1983). In another study, 51 percent of mentoring relationships were initiated during graduate school (Knox and McGovern 1988); another documents that graduate school protégés who have had strong collaborative relationships with their mentors tended to achieve an academic position (Long and McGinnis 1985).

In a study of both female and male academic mentors, protégés whose careers paralleled those of their mentors were identified as the most successful (Blackburn, Chapman, and Cameron 1981). Additionally, mentors promoted individuals most like themselves—their clones.

Conceptual models for mentoring future teachers have been widely discussed. Numerous studies and research articles have noted the advantages of mentoring in the K–12 setting; in fact, an entire issue of *The Journal of Teacher Education* (American Association 1992) was devoted to induction and mentoring. Mentoring in elementary and secondary education has focused on the development of teachers' professionalism, and some researchers have suggested that mentor programs may increase the retention rate of teachers and improve the quality of their instruction (see, e.g., Galvez-Hjornevik 1985).

Other evidence exists of differences between mentoring in academe and in business and industry (Luna and Cullen 1994b). Interviews with 51 female executives/administrators regarding their experiences as a mentor or protégé found that mentoring in education included both professional and personal mentoring goals, while in business and industry, it encompassed only professional or career-oriented mentoring activities, with an organizational focus as the primary function of the women's mentoring experiences. Women mentors and protégés in business and industry were less willing to enter into informal, personal mentoring situations than women in higher education.

Some researchers have found that business and industry is preoccupied with competencies and associated performance standards and assessment criteria (Caldwell and Carter 1993); that is, it has a concern for product and measurable outcomes, which in turn affects approaches to mentoring. This concern is not as evident in educational settings, where the focus is more on process and the collaborative culture.

Benefits of Mentoring in the Workplace

Studies have suggested numerous benefits of mentoring to the protégé, the mentor, and the organization. Through mentoring, protégés gain an understanding of the organizational culture (Kram 1986), have access to informal networks of communication that carry significant professional information (Olian et al. 1988), and receive assistance and support in defining and reaching career aspirations (Bogat and Redner 1985). These advantages have been similar in both education and noneducation settings.

Mentors gain satisfaction from assisting junior colleagues, at the same time improving their own managerial skills; additionally, mentors are the beneficiaries of increased stimulation by the ideas of bright and creative protégés (Reich 1986).

Mentoring has proved valuable to the overall stability and health of an organization. It plays a vital role in future organizational leadership, and the development of potential leaders is strengthened with the nurturing of junior colleagues. Additionally, mentoring promotes progression in one's career, improves performance within a work group, and ensures that discrimination does not occur (Noe 1988; Reich 1986; Roche 1979).

MENTORING FRAMEWORKS

It is compelling to discover that life cycle theorists had powerful role models and mentors. Freud was a mentor to Erik Erikson, while Freud's and Erikson's frameworks and theories provided a foundation for the research of Daniel Levinson et al., *The Seasons of a Man's Life* (1978). Each of these theorists found that historical accounts and biographical methodologies were useful in the conceptualization of personality development and the identification of life stages or cycles. Kram (1986), building on these foundations, characterized a hierarchy of mentoring functions. Erikson, Levinson, and Kram each advanced primary developmental concepts central to the mentoring relationship (see table 2).

TABLE 2
COMPARISON OF MENTORING CONCEPTS

Mentoring Theorist	Framework	Key Characteristics And Descriptors
Erikson	Middle adulthood generativity carried out by caring for others through guiding future generations	Mature drive to generate altruistic and creative acts and nurture one's progeny through caring
Levinson	Mentoring a young adult in the occupational and social world by fostering the "Dream"; eventually followed by an inevitable parting of mentor and protégé	Mentoring functions include teaching skills and knowledge, sponsoring entry and advancement in an organization, guiding through complex occupational and social pathways.
Kram	Mentoring relationship consists of four phases: initiation, cultivation, separation, and redefinition.	Mentoring career functions: sponsorship, coaching, protection, exposure, and challenging work; psychosocial functions: role modeling, counseling, acceptance and confirmation, and friendship. When the full range of functions is experienced, greater intimacy exists.

Erikson's Stages

Erik Erikson is known for his work related to life stages (1963, p. 247). Erikson postulated that as an individual journeys through various psychosocial stages, an inner division develops. This division is defined by a crisis or critical steps between two forces in opposition to one another, such as Basic Trust versus Mistrust (stage 1) or Identity versus Role Confusion (stage 5). According to Erikson, the human personality matures as a new ego quality unfolds through the acquisition of a new strength. Additionally, each successive stage has a special relationship to a basic societal element.

In middle adulthood, the conflict of Generativity versus Stagnation (stage 7) occurs with the evolving strength or virtue of *care*. With regard to this stage, "Mature man needs to be needed, and maturity needs guidance as well as encouragement from what has been produced and must be taken care of" (Erikson 1963, p. 266). Guiding the next generation is the primary principle of generativity, generally manifested by one's relationship to one's children or progeny. Through generativity, care is concentrated on those one cares for or can take care of to the exclusion of all others (*Harvard Educational Review* 1981). Generativity is the basic building block of mentoring as one gives back or mentors a new generation. It can also be expressed in the wider sense of advancing altruistic and creative acts and ideals (Erikson 1978). It would be important as a mentor, for example, to provide opportunities for a junior colleague instead of only enhancing one's career.

Levinson's Seasons

Daniel Levinson, building on the works of Freud, Erikson, and Jung, used biographic methods to identify four overlapping eras of the life cycle, each lasting about 25 years. Through his study of 40 men with the occupations of hourly worker, executive, academic biologist, and novelist, he gave a focus to the time frame from the late teens to the late forties, and he identified the following life sequences:

1. Childhood and adolescence (birth to 22 years)
2. Early adulthood (17 to 45 years)
3. Middle adulthood (40 to 65 years)
4. Late adulthood (60 years to death).

Levinson noted that the mentor relationship is first realized during the "novice phase" of early adulthood. This relationship is extremely important and significant to a young man. The male mentor, several years older by at least half a generation, is a senior individual usually found in the young man's workplace. The mentor fosters the young adult's development by assisting his transition into adulthood and peer relationships. The most significant function of the relationship is to support and facilitate the young adult's *realization of the Dream*—an exciting vision of imagined possibilities in life. The mentor provides some critical support:

> *He fosters the young adult's development by believing in him, sharing the youthful Dream and giving it his blessing, helping to define the newly emerging self in its newly discovered world, and creating a space in which the young man can work on a reasonable satisfactory life structure that contains the Dream* (Levinson et al. 1978, p. 99).

The mentor's functions include teaching skills and knowledge, sponsoring entry and advancement, hosting or guiding the protégé through complex occupational or social paths, and inculcating cultural and organizational values and customs (Levinson et al. 1978). Additionally, the mentor serves as an exemplar and role model admired by his protégé, sought out during times of stress or when emotional support is necessary.

In Levinson's study, men had male mentors. In a good mentoring relationship, the mentor did not provide a paternal role or cause feelings of dependency as a father might encourage. As the protégé evolved to a more independent individual, he became autonomous and the relationship naturally shifted. In a difficult mentoring relationship, the mentor might fear the protégé and act out harmful behaviors. Over time, the mentor and protégé might benefit from this problematic relationship as a result of the give-and-take interchange. Even with problems within the mentoring relationship, mutual satisfaction can be derived. Although the mentoring relationship could last two or three years, it could possibly continue for as long as 10 years, with the separation potentially developing into a difficult and rocky conflict.

When a man in his late thirties gives up his mentor, his behavior signals that he is advancing into the period of "becoming one's own man" (Levinson et al. 1978). At this point, a difficult separation likened to the ending of a love relationship ensues. The protégé might develop intense feelings of bitterness toward what he now considers an overbearing and demanding mentor. The mentor might believe his protégé to be touchy and unappreciative. According to Levinson's research, a man's struggle with his mentor centers on the rejection of the relationship—not because it is difficult or harmful but because it has served its purpose. Over time, the pair might form a warm friendship, but like a love affair, much of its intrinsic value and usefulness is put into perspective only after the termination of the relationship.

A man in middle adulthood serving as a mentor can achieve great satisfaction. Mentoring serves the adult need to nurture others' lives and is represented through altruistic behaviors. Along these same lines, the mentor passes on his knowledge and skills, strengthening his sense of self and allowing him to fulfill his passion to be needed.

Some adults do not give or receive mentoring (Levinson et al. 1978). While mentoring can be a special gift to the recipient, organization, or society at large, mentor relationships can be stifled by limitations of individual development or organizational structures. To build a cadre of mentors in an organization, special support and encouragement should be fostered toward those individuals nearing the middle adult years. And the lack of mentoring is a waste of talent and an impediment to social change (Levinson et al. 1978, p. 334).

Kram's Theories

Kram (1983) characterized the phases of a mentoring relationship through her study of mentor-protégé pairs in an organizational setting. Although these developmental relationships averaged five years in length, they comprised four distinct phases. The beginning mentoring period, in which the senior individual is respected and admired and the junior colleague is considered coachable, is termed the *initiation period*. As the relationship progresses during the *cultivation period,* the protégé can experience a full interchange of career and psychosocial functions. The peak of the developmental process occurs during this time as the junior colleague acquires important technical skills and learns the ropes of the workplace. The protégé also gains self-esteem and is able to confirm a chosen organizational identity and his or her goals.

As the value of the mentoring relationship matures and is assessed over time, the junior colleague exerts independence and autonomy. This *separation period* can be a time of loss, anxiety, and turmoil as the protégé endeavors to "come of age" by separating from the mentor both emotionally and organizationally. Finally, during the *redefinition period,* the relationship may welcome a more equal footing. The mentor can enjoy the protégé's accomplishments, and a collegial friendship may ensue. Conversely, hostility and resentment may exist as the mentor appears disinterested and the former protégé likens this behavior to abandonment. During the redefinition period, the relationship is viewed positively or negatively as one that is no longer needed or desired.

Kram's definition of mentoring functions centers around two rubrics (see table 3). First, career functions permit the protégé to acquire new knowledge and to grow within the organizational structure. Second, the psychosocial functions advance a growing trust and intimacy between the pair by providing enhanced identity, continuing support, and the sharing of dilemmas.

The career functions of sponsorship, coaching, protection, exposure, and challenging work provide developmental levels of support that are less intimate than the psychosocial functions. Relationships that primarily advance these functions are valued for their work-related values and the institutional ends that they serve (Kram 1986).

The psychosocial functions of role modeling, counseling, acceptance and confirmation, and friendship allow social interaction, greater interaction, and familiarity. Which functions are provided in a mentoring relationship are determined by interpersonal skills, individual needs, and the organizational environment (Kram 1985). Additionally, concerns about self, career, and family confound the extent of the functions experienced.

The range of functions experienced is a result of primary or secondary mentorship. In a primary mentorship, both career and psychosocial functions are practiced. These pri-

TABLE 3
MENTORING FUNCTIONS

Career Functions

Sponsorship
Opening doors. Having connections that will support the junior's career advancement.

Coaching
Teaching "the ropes." Giving relevant positive and negative feedback to improve the junior's performance and potential.

Protection
Providing support in different situations. Taking responsibility for mistakes that were outside the junior's control. Acting as a buffer when necessary.

Exposure
Creating opportunities for the junior to demonstrate competence where it counts. Taking the junior to important meetings that will enhance his or her visibility.

Challenging Work
Delegating assignments that stretch the junior's knowledge and skills in order to stimulate growth and preparation to move ahead.

Psychosocial Functions

Role Modeling
Demonstrating valued behavior, attitudes, and/or skills that aid the junior in achieving competence, confidence, and a clear professional identity.

Counseling
Providing a helpful and confidential forum for exploring personal and professional dilemmas. Excellent listening, trust, and rapport that enable both individuals to address central developmental concerns.

Acceptance and Confirmation
Providing ongoing support, respect, and admiration, which strengthens self-confidence and self-image. Regularly reinforcing both are highly valued people and contributors to the organization.

Friendship
Mutual caring and intimacy that extends beyond the requirements of daily work tasks. Sharing of experience outside the immediate work setting.

Source: Kram 1986, p. 162. Reproduced by permission.

mary mentors are viewed as unselfish and altruistic—most generative and caring (as in the Eriksonian sense). Subsequently, secondary mentors advance only career functions. With secondary mentorship, a businesslike relationship enhances the career goals of mentor and protégé.

Great value can be derived from the relationship constellation (Kram 1985, 1986). This concept promotes a range of relationships with superiors, peers, subordinates, family, and friends that supports and encourages an individual's development. "The concept of a relationship constellation eliminates the misconception that mentoring is embodied in one hierarchical relationship" (Kram 1986, p. 174). Furthermore, several types of peer relationships can be identified that have distinctive career or psychosocial characteristics (Kram 1985). For each peer relationship, the level of commitment, intensity, shared issues, and needs satisfied may vary and change. Peer relationships allow support and opportunities for growth through the development of successive career stages (see figure 1). These relationships are valuable mentoring alternatives (Kram 1985).

FIGURE 1
A CONTINUUM OF PEER RELATIONSHIPS

Information Peer	Collegial Peer	Special Peer
Primary Function	*Primary Functions*	*Primary Functions*
Information Sharing	Career Strategizing Job-related Feedback Friendship	Confirmation Emotional Support Personal Feedback Friendship

Source: Kram and Isabella 1985, p. 119. Reproduced by permission.

Mentor-Protégé Roles
The application of theoretical frameworks can readily support the role of the mentor or the role of the protégé. The mentor will express a desire to pass on the torch to a new generation—a developmental tendency that organizations should foster (Erikson 1963). Levinson et al. (1978) expanded this notion by defining the phases of life sequences and by pairing mentoring phenomena with the middle years of adulthood. The role of mentor is further defined through

activities in the workplace, by passing on knowledge and skills, and through emotional support (Levinson et al. 1978). Kram (1983) characterized these environmental and emotional functions and extended the work of Erikson and Levinson by clarifying the stages of the mentoring relationship. Kram's functions define a hierarchy by which mentors and protégés can map developmental progress.

These three mentoring frameworks are the primary guideposts from which mentoring models were developed. Mentors and protégés can gauge the progress of their relationship by comparing it to those described by Levinson or Kram. Protégés might consider recruiting among desirable mentors according to characteristics outlined in these studies. Indeed, the protégé could attain a deeper understanding of what occurs naturally within the mentoring dyad through attention to research on and theories of mentoring. For example, does the mentor provide an opportunity for more challenging work, thereby offering exposure to organizational authorities? Conversely, does the mentor sponsor the protégé in a manner that limits career possibilities? The plausible scenarios for protégés and mentors are too numerous to delineate here, but mentors and protégés alike should heighten their awareness of the positives and negatives that accompany the mentoring relationship.

Mentoring and Caring

The central theme of caring defines the role of the mentor in the works of Erikson, Levinson, and Kram. The mentor cares through demonstrated behaviors, actions, and characteristics. This caring, more senior individual guides, encourages, parents, makes sacrifices for, fosters, connects with, supports, and befriends the protégé.

These actions could occur in both the work-related and personal lives of the mentor and the protégé. The concept of caring for the protégé may at first encompass career functions or technical knowledge and aspects of mentoring. As the relationship matures, the interpersonal nature of caring is expressed. This significant event empowers the protégé and permits a stronger bond to be realized. As the full range of support is expressed, greater intimacy and satisfaction are experienced in the mentoring relationship.

The seminal works of Erikson, Levinson, and Kram regarding mentoring frameworks have provided foundations for mentoring programs, models, and strategies found in academe and business and industry today. Moreover, these frameworks and conceptualizations continue to denote a primary infrastructure of care and empowerment.

MENTORING AND FACULTY DEVELOPMENT

The concepts, practices, and programs of mentoring are advocated and practiced frequently in higher education. Educational administrators in the form of college vice presidents, deans, and other academic leaders mentor leadership. Translating knowledge to practice is somewhat difficult for the professoriat, because the profession lacks the structure for inculcating the ideals necessary to transform new leadership. Thus, a review of mentoring and leadership may guide faculty and administrators in rediscovering mentoring as a strategy for enhancing faculty careers.

The Progression of the Mentoring Relationship

A natural developmental interaction generally occurs between the mentor and protégé that will allow a mentoring relationship to persist. First, the mentor notices the protégé because the protégé has achieved something, enhancing his or her visibility. Second, the mentor may test or watch the potential protégé to determine whether future contributions are viable or special attributes are present. After recruiting the protégé, the mentor cultivates the relationship. At this time, a closer working status might exist that allows for daily contact between the mentoring dyad, which bestows special status on the protégé by association with the senior mentor with access to an inner circle of institutional gatekeepers. Through this new venue, the mentee views and has access to a larger scope of the institution and acquires knowledge. The work of the protégé may take on special significance that enhances the careers of both protégé and mentor.

As the relationship develops, the mentor may cultivate the protégé's leadership or ability through example, opportunities for practice, or direction. If leadership is the goal, the leadership mentor may concentrate on three major responsibilities:

1. Teaching the standards (written and unwritten) related to professional behavior and performance;
2. Developing trust in the protégé and establishing the reliability and predictability of the working relationship;
3. Maintaining a major influence in the selection and/or development of leaders.

Because many of the policies and decisions made by faculty leaders in colleges and universities have long-lasting and financial implications, mentors desire positive outcomes when delegating major responsibilities to protégés. For this reason, trust and predictability are major developmental considerations that herald the dyadic bond. The incremental hierarchical mentoring functions established by Kram (1986) are in essence opportunities to formulate and judge the protégé's ability to handle difficult dilemmas. For example, the protégé learns the ropes before accepting challenging work or assignments that demonstrate his or her competence (Kram 1986). Testing of the mentoring relationship and the protégé can occur and intensify over time. Through faculty development, an improved organizational culture is more likely, which can be viewed as an improved congruence among the organizational structure, process, strategy, and people, as well as enhancement of the organization's capacity for self-renewal (Beer 1980).

To translate knowledge into practice and advance the academic culture and leadership skills for faculty, mentoring goals, direction, and outcomes need to be determined. The following descriptors may provide basic building blocks for faculty and leadership development (Daloz 1986; Zuckerman 1970):

- *Teacher:* One who shares the tacit and technical knowledge of the professional field, the environment, and the institutional social and political culture and climate ("what matters") and demonstrates accepted and valued behaviors and attitudes within the profession and institution ("what's important").
- *Enhancer:* One who supports, sponsors, and stimulates the protégé in terms of professional advancement, uses the mentor's connections to promote and create opportunities, assists in identifying and clarifying the protégé's needs and goals, and prepares the protégé for professional growth inside and outside the organization.
- *Caretaker:* One who provides advice, assistance, and guidance on a more personal level; nurtures and reinforces the protégé's identity, including self-confidence and self-image; and befriends and counsels the protégé within the sphere of like problems and goals.
- *Modeling:* An identification process that occurs in the mentor relationship whereby the protégé sees personality traits, skills, and/or knowledge in the mentor that he or she desires.

- *Maintaining tradition:* A knowledge or information process whereby the mentor provides a base for the protégé, passing on or handing down the tradition of inquiry and sharing how to acquire critical information.
- *Offering a map:* A planning process whereby the mentor assists the protégé in developing a plan for the future and determining ways or methods of achieving desired goals.
- *Conceptualizing:* A process to assist the protégé in searching for new ways to think about or conceptualize teaching and learning in the academy.
- *Providing a mirror:* A process of increasing the protégé's self-awareness by giving feedback to assess thinking and development.

Faculty Career Development

Mentoring has shown promise as an appropriate intervention for addressing a variety of faculty needs over academic careers (Diehl and Simpson 1989). Human resource development, emphasizing the professional and personal needs of new faculty, has used the concepts of mentoring to assist with teaching duties and effectiveness. In a large study (Queralt 1982), faculty with mentors demonstrated greater productivity as leaders in professional associations, received more competitive grants, and published more books and articles than those faculty without mentors. These thriving faculty indicated greater career and job satisfaction and achieved more success than did their mentorless counterparts. Moreover, faculty used more than one mentor, and they appeared to progress farther in their careers (Queralt 1982). These findings correlate well with the concept of the relationship constellation, defined as multiple mentors assisting with different aspects of career and personal development (Kram 1986, p. 174).

In an interesting comparison of mentoring functions among protégés in formal and informal mentoring relationships and nonmentored individuals, informally mentored protégés received more career-related mentoring and higher pay than protégés in facilitated programs (Chao, Walz, and Gardner 1992; see also Roche 1979). Moreover, mentored individuals reported greater job satisfaction and organizational socialization (job outcomes).

A program designed to facilitate junior faculty as change leaders and to advance a discipline or profession reveals 10

Mentoring has shown promise as an appropriate intervention for addressing a variety of faculty needs over academic careers.

key principles for effective mentoring (Chalmers 1992, p. 72). These principles may be particularly useful as a framework for mentoring faculty's leadership:

1. Previously developed habits of work and thought will be influential. Junior faculty should be encouraged to advance vision, focus priorities, write for conceptualizing, exhibit respect, and share credit for positive outcomes.
2. Balance and harmony between personal and professional life are essential.
3. Exercising self-discipline on accepted responsibilities is encouraged. Junior faculty need vision and focus on priorities, therefore not becoming overburdened by multiple tasks.
4. Accountability for personal performance is promoted. Junior faculty should not accept mediocrity from themselves because they have voluntarily taken on additional assignments.
5. Be open to learning from personal experiences. Reflection on difficult assignments or failures can result in personal growth.
6. Understand and cooperate with forces of change. Faculty should consider integrating forces of change into personal goals and objectives to ameliorate barriers to success.
7. A vision or mission is the framework that relates one's efforts to one another. Faculty should consider the interrelatedness of personal, departmental, and institutional goals to focus their efforts.
8. Appreciate constituencies. Junior faculty should develop an appreciation of groups or individuals who operate through the system.
9. Progress is an incremental, iterative process. Career development depends on growth in vision, focus on priorities, and the ability to develop goals.
10. Mentoring is important to receive at all stages of adult growth. Faculty should take the opportunity to learn from caring and wiser persons.

Other researchers have determined the influence of a mentor on career development, publications, grant productivity, collaborations, professional networks, and job placement of protégés (Blackburn, Chapman, and Cameron 1981; Cameron and Blackburn 1981). Mentoring has been used to enhance the development of junior faculty or part-time instructors or for specific purposes, such as research and scholarship development (Bergen and Connelly 1988; Campbell 1992; Chalmers 1992). In one study, the mentor's role as collaborator appeared to greatly influence the protégé's number of publications when the bond was formed during doctoral study (Long and McGinnis 1985). For the students in that study, the mentor's performance was a significant factor for indicating the level of prestige for later academic appointments, thereby affecting both achievement and ascription in the academic arena. "The ascriptive advantages of one's mentor are then drawn upon and enhanced though the joint effects of reinforcement and context. This . . . is how cumulative advantage operates" (p. 279).

A study of the nature of mentoring among faculty at a large public university analyzed a total of 29 activities denoting four primary types of mentoring functions (Sands, Parson, and Duane 1991). A *friend* allowed emotional support, social interactions, and advice with personal problems. The *career guide* emphasized professional advancement, while the *information source* provided policies and procedures related to promotion, committee expectations, or other responsibilities. The *intellectual guide* promoted collaboration and constructive feedback. As a result of this analysis, faculty were aware of the type of mentoring they desired or preferred to extend.

Mentoring new faculty should result in several suggested general outcomes (Boice 1992). The findings of that study indicate that:

1. Arbitrarily paired mentors and protégés worked as well as traditional pairs. It was successful because the information shared was survivalistic in nature and basic to progress, regardless of the department.
2. Mentors and protégés from the same department worked at least as well as those from different departments. Protégés in different disciplines were more open with their mentors, and the mentors and protégés together were able to deal with department-specific expectations.
3. Frequent reminders to meet regularly helped ensure the pair's bonding. Mentoring dyads completed checklists and issued ratings related to involvement.

4. Most mentoring pairs left to themselves displayed disappointingly narrow styles. Those who shared experiences with others initiated new avenues.
5. Mentors assumed the role of interventionist with reluctance. They did not want to interfere with classroom teaching experiences (pp. 52–54).

Alternatives to mentoring, such as faculty peer mentoring, can be a powerful intervention strategy for the improvement of instruction. In one study, the assignment of a peer mentor, with delineated outcomes, resulted in improved teaching for inexperienced or stagnated faculty as well as a sharing of disciplined-related knowledge, teaching strategies, and ideas (Harnish and Wild 1993). Faculty members were also able to improve and upgrade content knowledge and keep skills current while revising instructional materials for students. Moreover, cross-discipline approaches to solving problems and collaboration resulted in renewed professional growth and teaching effectiveness. Another alternative, committee mentoring, offers support and direction for the protégé and clarifies expectations (Boice 1992).

Most faculty-to-faculty mentoring occurs informally. If planned, the mentoring program is usually designed for new or junior faculty. For example, 74 percent of new faculty in a facilitated mentoring program at the University of Albany rated the program as "significant." In the same program, an even larger percentage of mentors recognized the program's importance (Xu and Newman 1986).

The flip side of promoting faculty mentoring is the sink-or-swim approach or the no-one-helped-me attitude:

Most newly appointed assistant professors have a general idea what being a professor is all about, or at least what they think it entails. But since there's no West Point for professors, real training for the assignment comes from being in the assignment. So they learn from role models and from making their own mistakes (Schoenfeld and Magnan 1992, p. 1).

The basic, but frequently overlooked, elements necessary for new faculty's success include involvement, regimen, solving the right problems, and social networking

(Boice 1992). A balance of this approach to faculty development ensures a good start and promotes desirable outcomes.

Central to strong development are administrative support, good management, orientation toward the future, and collegiality (Jarvis 1992). All the ingredients must be present to form the desired product. For instance, collegiality is an "important single factor in faculty development" (Jarvis 1992, p. 65). This sense of friendship, support, belonging, and encouragement—that is, caring and mentoring—can provide an environment where professionals can flourish. Without this simple element of collegiality, productivity will be diminished.

These same principles are important for developing leadership. Table 4 lists the advantages of faculty leadership.

TABLE 4

ADVANTAGES OF MENTORING FACULTY LEADERS

- Enhances organizational culture (department, college, institution)
- Clarifies internal academic politics
- Allows for continuity about the institution and its people
- Promotes problem solving
- Provides for the maturation of personal judgment (how to judge people, control anger, or analyze issues)
- Cultivates contacts and networks with colleagues
- Heightens competence and productivity
- Fosters empowerment
- Advances career development and planning
- Creates social change
- Supports opportunities to improve diversity
- Favors optimal use of human potential and resources
- Attracts and retains good faculty
- Improves career and personal satisfaction
- Nourishes rejuvenation
- Encourages opportunities, options, and alternatives
- Promotes role identification
- Plans for succession
- Increases the number of ambassadors for the institution

Empowerment and Mentoring

A major element of excellence in an organization is the empowerment of its individuals. For example, by permitting faculty to creatively participate in projects, governance, and problem solving, the institution will improve and succeed as it works to achieve its mission. As the mentoring relationship grows from a directive interaction to that equivalent of collaboration, transmission of the professional legacy to posterity occurs by empowerment of the protégé (Healy and Welchert 1990).

This ideal is modeled through a five-level process (Gray 1989a). In the Mentor/Protégé Relationship Model, the mentor works toward improving the protégé's learning outcomes related to personal and cognitive skills and attitudes. At level 1 or 2, the protégé might depend on the mentor, who offers advice and solutions to problems. As the protégé advances toward independence (level 5), the mentor adopts a "backseat" approach to coaching and feedback. By being aware of where the mentoring relationship lies, the mentor can offer appropriate guidance. Eventually, the authority to make decisions and to act without approval evolves for the protégé, who becomes empowered.

Several major components are necessary for empowerment (Lloyd and Berthelot 1992). First is trust in others, for without trust in the abilities, intelligence, loyalty, and motivation of one's colleagues, empowerment will not evolve. Self-empowered individuals additionally exhibit self-esteem, which can be expressed as confidence, a positive self-image, or determination. A mentor who displays high levels of self-esteem and confidence does not depend upon the approval of others and might take more risks in his or her role as leader. A protégé notes this self-empowering characteristic through his or her mentor's role-modeling behaviors. Further important aspects of self-empowerment are positive expectations and attitudes and the effective interaction with others. A protégé develops these skills by observing the mentor's actions and through practice when delegated challenging work or given opportunities. "The way to achieve ultimate power as a manager is to give power to the people who work for you" (Tracy 1992, p. 161). Table 5 outlines 10 principles for empowering others.

Ultimately, self-empowerment denotes one's position and power. Sponsoring a protégé is a way of providing power to another person. In a study of sponsorship in a complex business organization, power was provided three ways (Kanter 1977). First, power was displayed by fighting for the protégé through the mentor's position. Second, power was

TABLE 5

TEN PRINCIPLES FOR EMPOWERING OTHERS

1. Tell people what their responsibilities are.
2. Give authority equal to the responsibilities assigned to them.
3. Set standards of excellence.
4. Provide training that will enable them to meet the standards.
5. Give knowledge and information.
6. Provide feedback on their performance.
7. Recognize their achievements.
8. Trust them.
9. Give permission to fail.
10. Treat them with dignity and respect.

Source: Tracy 1992.

used by helping the protégé bypass the organizational hierarchy. Third, the protégé was provided with reflected power derived from association with a competent and powerful mentor.

The ability to lead is achieved largely because an older, wiser, and more powerful mentor notes a spark of ability (leadership) and nurtures that potential (Moore 1982). Because leadership should not be left to chance, facilitated mentoring programs or planned mentoring tasks can be assigned, fostered, and evaluated. Mentoring should be viewed as important to the institution, and mentors should be regarded as valuable talent scouts and trainers. Potential new faculty leaders can be perceived as contributing something important to the organization other than the ordinary professional responsibilities. These contributions could involve risk taking that enhances the protégé's visibility.

Empowering faculty builds pride, responsibility, and growth and helps to clarify standards of excellence. Senior faculty can empower junior faculty by providing knowledge and feedback, and by establishing an environment that promotes trust, respect, and risk taking. This simple yet enlightening strategy is vital to the professoriat. Faculty leadership, development, and involvement are fostered through empowerment. In the end, the organization's effectiveness is advanced and students, faculty, and administrators benefit.

She earned a degree in the sciences and is employed in her first teaching position at a community college. After her first year at the college, she still does not understand the student evaluation policy, has questions about the content of her Biology I course, and cannot figure out why the process of requisitioning lab supplies takes so long. Another female professor has just completed her fifth year in a college of engineering at a major research university. She is concerned about the tenure process, as she plans to apply for tenure and promotion to associate professor the following year. Is her scholarship good enough? What about her evaluations from her department chair? Is there anything else she should be doing?

These two female educators could obviously benefit from a mentor. But mentoring can also play a role in assisting fatigued female senior faculty members and helping administrators who are concerned about using the talents of their female faculty more effectively. And what about educational institutions that are interested in recruiting more women and are concerned about increasing productivity with fewer resources? All of these issues relate to people and the work they do, and faculty's effectiveness and productivity can be addressed through mentoring strategies, tools, and plans. Mentoring in the workplace can address women's personal and professional needs. Moreover, the mentoring of female faculty members empowers these professionals, enabling them to develop their special skills and qualities.

Women's Experiences

It is only within the last decade that mentoring in relation to women's life cycles and development has been examined; major works of research on adult development focused on the eras and periods in the life cycle of males. More recently, new insights into the understanding of human development have been presented through descriptive and ethnographic accounts of women's experiences. Although the importance of mentoring in adult development was manifested in the works of Levinson et al. (1978) and Erikson (1963), life cycle theorists traditionally described mentoring as paternalistic, as men were the subjects of study.

Women in business and academe inevitably have different experiences in their professions by virtue of their social status and cultural experiences (Swoboda and Millar 1986).

Therefore, a new understanding of women's experiences was necessary (see, e.g., Bardwick 1980; Carlson 1972; Faver 1980; Gilligan 1982; Katz 1979; and Kram 1985).

Women are changing the fabric of the workforce. In 1988, 51.7 million women aged 16 to 64 were employed or looking for work (National Commission 1989). One year later, the number had increased to 56 million women, and 20 percent of managerial positions were held by women (National Commission 1990). It is projected that 61.5 percent of all females, the fasting-growing segment of the workforce in the United States, will be employed in 2000 (Bureau of Labor 1992).

By the 21st century:

- Eighty percent of women aged 25 to 34 will be in the labor force.
- The number of Hispanic women in the labor force will increase from 3.8 million to 5.8 million.
- The number of African-American women in the job market will increase by 33 percent, to more than 8 million.
- One in 10 new women entrants to the labor force will be Asian, American Indian, or Native Alaskan (National Commission 1990).

Although these statistics reflect the growing presence of women in the workforce, certain research shows that entering the labor market and climbing the career ladder are two different matters. For example, a recent survey based on a national sample of both large and small organizations found that over 50 percent of companies experienced moderate to great difficulty in attracting and retaining women managers (Rosen, Miguel, and Peirce 1989; see also Morrison, White, Van Velsor, and Center for Creative Leadership 1992). Over 65 percent of these companies noted the absence of mentors as a major problem encountered by female employees. This finding supports prior research (Warihay 1980) in which the 2,000 female managers surveyed noted the absence of mentors in their career progression. A study conducted by the New York executive search firm Korn/Ferry International and the UCLA Graduate School of Management (1990) found that women held fewer than 5 percent of all senior management positions.

The now well-documented "glass ceiling" [is] a barrier

so subtle that it is transparent, yet so strong that it prevents women . . . from moving beyond middle management. . . . The organizational forces that create and maintain these kinds of invisible walls and ceilings are likely reflected in the [absence of a] mentoring process and its goals (Gilbert and Rossman 1992, p. 234).

Some women do not enter into a mentoring relationship, either as a mentor or a protégé. Several possible reasons exist:

1. The lack of appropriate female role models limits women's career advancement.
2. Women may develop social skills related to career enhancement much later than men, thus inhibiting opportunities to develop mentoring relationships.
3. Some women prefer to be the "queen bee" and are threatened by talented junior colleagues.
4. The male-female mentoring relationship keeps men from becoming mentors to aspiring women because of potential sexual tensions and suspicions.
5. Men do not always perceive women as serious about career development (Bolton 1980, pp. 203–4).

Women are more likely to believe that hard work, perseverance, and skills are the primary determinants in climbing the career ladder and therefore less likely to be concerned about finding a mentor (Nieva and Gutek 1981; see also Ragins 1989). Additionally, female workers expect to find mentors in their senior male colleagues, who hold the majority of influential positions. In a recent study, women in both business and education noted that their mentors had been male, either older male employees or fathers (Luna and Cullen 1994a), but these same women noted that finding a mentor is not guaranteed in any work environment.

Research points to greater job success and job satisfaction for women with one or more mentors (Dreher and Ash 1990; Michael 1992; Riley and Wrench 1985). Female protégés specifically reported elevated self-confidence, enhanced opportunities for creativity, and increased development of skills (Reich 1986). Female employees without mentors are less effective on the job (Ilgen and Youtz 1986; Martinko and Gardner 1982). "Taking advantage of talent by

Research points to greater job success and job satisfaction for women with one or more mentors.

providing training, support, and mentoring to both men and women simply serves the interests" of an organization (Dreher and Ash 1990, p. 544).

What's Different for Women Faculty

The number of female students at U.S. colleges and universities continues to grow. Eighty-two percent of the increase in enrollments from 1991 to 1992 comprised women, and females accounted for 55 percent of all students in fall 1992 (Shea 1994). Women earned 54 percent of master's degrees in 1992 but only 37 percent of doctoral degrees (*Chronicle* 1994). And fewer female and minority students are selecting higher education as a career (Parsons 1992).

Full-time female faculty members in public and private four-year colleges and universities continue to make less money as professors, associate professors, assistant professors, instructors, and lecturers (Leatherman 1995). In 1994–95, 36.5 percent of faculty held the rank of full professor, with women representing only 5.9 percent of this percentage (Leatherman 1995). A salary survey conducted by the College and University Personnel Association found that the lowest-paid faculty positions in higher education were in those fields dominated by women (Magner 1994). Thus, increasing the number of female faculty members in colleges and universities is necessary to provide appropriate support and role modeling for the increasing number of female students.

Other concerns exist for female faculty members. For example, junior female faculty are more likely to leave higher education before tenure decisions and are less likely to receive tenure (see, e.g., Rausch, Ortiz, Douthitt, and Reed 1989). Women report greater social and intellectual isolation in higher education (Clark and Corcoran 1986; Yoder 1985) and are less likely to be integrated into networks that allocate resources and provide academic opportunities (Johnsrud and Wunsch 1991). Moreover, female faculty members are less likely than men to receive counteroffers in salary and benefits from their home institutions when seeking employment elsewhere (Commission on the Status 1990).

Several factors are important in the promotion and tenure of faculty:

1. *Custom and preference,* defined as the "absence of clear and universally agreed-upon formal standards, use of

ambiguous criteria, and closed, confidential decision making" (Exum, Menges, Watkins, and Berglund 1984, p. 305).

2. *Merit,* explained in terms of emphasis on research, scholarship, and good teaching.
3. *Collegiality and consensus,* interpreted as the importance of being liked, emphasizing that custom and preference and merit realistically are not the only criteria used in making decisions about tenure and promotion (Exum et al. 1984; Menges and Exum 1983).

Moreover, research suggests that these features of the academic environment produce a situation in which mentors can assist in providing access to information networks and opportunities that can help female faculty members deal with those factors critical to their promotion and tenure (see also Cullen and Luna 1993).

Similar factors influence the promotion of females, with career progression characterized as being influenced by both intrinsic factors (personal and professional) and extrinsic factors (organizational and interpersonal) (Madsen and Blide 1992). "The interaction between these factors is often driven by gender differences allowing men to progress and succeed, whereas women remain beneath the glass ceiling" (p. 54). Perhaps continuing education and opportunities for mentoring would promote the integration of women in the workforce (Madsen and Blide 1992). Academic women are empowered through relationships with mentors who have professional authority, organization authority, professional influence, and organization influence (Nichols, Carter, and Golden 1985).

Less valued than research and other scholarly activities, teaching has become a commanding obligation for female faculty in higher education. Women generally have increased teaching loads and greater numbers of student advisees (Carnegie Foundation 1989; Strathan, Richardson, and Cook 1991). Although women note their teaching and interaction with students as stimulating and satisfying, heavy teaching assignments inhibit female faculty's productivity in research (Association of American Colleges 1983; Maack and Passet 1994).

Some researchers have called the mentoring of female faculty members a validation process of acceptance into the collegial network that governs tenure, promotion, workload, and recognition. Mentoring assists the protégé in seeing herself as "a member of the profession, encouraging and fostering a self-image as a legitimate member of the community of scholars" (Simeone 1987, p. 101).

Same-Sex/Cross-Gender Mentoring

A study of women in academe found that 66 percent of female administrators had mentors in their work setting (Knox and McGovern 1988). A study of mentoring at a large research institution, however, noted that the largest activity related to mentoring occurred during graduate school and that only one-third of the faculty reported having a mentor from the same university (Sands, Parson, and Duane 1991). Most studies concluded that male mentors are more readily available for female faculty or for female graduate students. On the other hand, women recognized other significant support persons, such as mothers, fathers, and husbands (see, e.g., Astin and Leland 1991; Luna and Cullen 1994a). Because fewer women are in administrative or senior faculty roles in education, these women note several limitations in mentoring junior faculty members (see table 6).

Female faculty members note that mentoring was important "in easing their adjustment to the academic environment and helping them advance their career" (Maack and Passet 1994, p. 88). The same participants in the study, however, emphasized the need for female mentors who had been able to integrate their personal and professional lives. This need included mentors who were married and parents, and who juggled household responsibilities. Male mentors for female professionals could provide a narrower range of benefits for women, as they might have experienced different impacts of organizational practices and different experiences regarding the integration of work and family (Gilbert and Rossman 1992). Additionally, men might have less patience in mentoring female faculty members who have less time to contribute to scholarly endeavors (Cordova, Neely, and Shaughnessay 1988). Male faculty members may avoid choosing female protégés because of the "overvisibility factor" (that is, women's mistakes are often loudly broadcast, which might damage male colleagues' reputations) and concerns about rumors of sexual involvement (Association of American Colleges 1983; see also Ragins 1989).

TABLE 6

A MODEL OF OPERATIONAL LIMITATIONS FOR WOMEN MENTORS

Limitations	Description and Characteristics
Oversubscription	Limited number of senior women characterized by high mentor-protégé ratios. Few senior women in midmanagement and fewer in high administrative positions.
Time	Senior women serving in multiple capacities and functions. Frequently must represent the female perspective in meetings and committees so has less time available to accomplish other tasks. Mentoring becomes lesser priority.
Caretaking	Inability to spend time away from workplace to assist junior colleagues because of responsibilities to family; constantly balancing work and home.
Hindering	Lack of camaraderie and interest in mentoring. Construction of barriers and feelings of competitiveness and jealousy toward junior women.
Naiveté	Uninformed about functions and importance of mentoring. Limited understanding of the significance of role modeling for junior women. Unsure of role in mentoring others.
Organizational	Institutional barriers and constraints related to time, financial, political, cultural, and gender insensitivity. Poor administrative or human resource focus and development.

Source: Luna and Cullen 1994a.

Numerous research studies have recommended that same-sex/same-race mentoring relationships be cultivated, if at all possible (see, e.g., Association of American Colleges 1983; Noe 1988; Shakeshaft 1987).

Women who mentor women, in comparison with male mentors, may see the relationships less related to the preservation of a social order in which they are either one-up or one-down and more related to the development of a network characterized by confirmation and support.

*Such views would be consistent with emerging definitions
of psychological empowerment as occurring through a
mutual, relational process and involving the motivation,
freedom, and capacity to act purposefully, with the mobi-
lization of the energies, resources, strengths, or powers of
each person* (Gilbert and Rossman 1992, p. 236).

The lack of senior women on campuses, however, may
preclude the possibility of junior female faculty members'
having mentors of the same sex. The dilemma of fewer
female mentors is exacerbated by differing workloads for
females in terms of committee assignments, scholarship,
teaching, and other responsibilities.

Considerations for Women Faculty
Female faculty members may need support in different areas
from male colleagues. Mentoring is important for women for
the following reasons:

- To validate a woman's sense of self-worth
- To provide support and direction
- To serve the diverse needs of women
- To help women develop new skills
- To help women think creatively about their futures
- To help women who need help
- To teach women how to network
- To give women the opportunity to mentor
- To help women overcome hurdles to promotion
- To focus on positive solutions
- To help women overcome psychological misconceptions
- To help women to enhance career-building skills
- To help women promote themselves and their careers
  (Barowsky 1988, pp. 36–37).

A mentoring program for probationary female faculty at a
large public research institution, drawing on the connection
between institutional climate and women's careers, developed the following goals for women: (1) to provide orientation to the institution and the academic culture, (2) to
develop personal and political skills for career development,
(3) to identity and use a network of senior colleagues, and
(4) to effect institutional change through the retention and
promotion of women faculty. The results of the mentoring
program showed that all the women remained at the univer-

sity, all first-year appointees had positive evaluations for their probationary contract renewals, and 91 percent of the females in the study continued in the mentoring program for another year (Wunsch 1993).

Some researchers have recommended that different mentoring strategies be used for special groups of female faculty members. For example, female professors in nontraditional academic disciplines, such as mathematics, business, engineering, and the sciences, could have a variety of personal and professional concerns that need to be addressed (Association of American Colleges 1983, p. 7). Issues to take into consideration are female faculty members' being in a nontraditional career that runs counter to social norms and not having access to a variety of institutional and other resources (e.g., labs, equipment, or funding for special research) to pursue basic work. Female faculty in nontraditional disciplines also need to be kept informed about new developments in the field.

"Clearly, advancing academic women and developing an equitable institutional climate and support system are closely linked. An emergent strategy to meet the needs of both individual faculty development and the redirection of the institutional support system is mentoring" (Wunsch 1993, p. 353). It is clear from the literature that more research needs to be conducted regarding mentoring female faculty, both personally and professionally.

MENTORING MINORITY FACULTY IN ACADEME

The academic community has been committed to increasing the number of minority faculty members, and efforts continue to recruit faculty members to more accurately reflect the demographics of society and the increasing enrollment of minority students in higher education. Professional organizations are concerned about disproportionately low numbers of minority faculty; for example, the American Association of University Professors has issued policy statements supporting programs to improve the participation of minority faculty at all levels of education.

The U.S. Department of Education reports the following percentages of academic degrees conferred by racial and ethnic group for 1991–92 (numbers rounded) (*Chronicle* 1994, p. A31):

	American Indian	Asian	African-American	Hispanic	White
Associate	0.8	3	8	6	82
Bachelor's	0.5	4	7	4	85
Master's	0.4	4	6	3	87
Doctorate	0.4	5	4	3	87

College enrollments of minorities have increased since 1976 (only African-American enrollments decreased from 1982 to 1986). In 1993, the Department of Education reported the following percentages of total enrollment for minority-group students (*Chronicle* 1995):

American Indian	Asian	African-American	Hispanic	White
0.9	5.1	9.9	6.9	77.2

The diversity of students is expected to continue to increase through the 21st century (see, e.g., National Center for Education Statistics 1994). And by "providing minority students with similar-race role models and . . . having such role models provide multiracial perspectives in the appropriate disciplines, the interests, motivation, and success of minority students will be enhanced" (Solmon and Wingard 1991, p. 33).

Interestingly, the percentages of full-time faculty members represented in colleges and universities as of SY 1991–92 do not proportionately reflect the diversity in enrollments (*Chronicle* 1994, p. A33):

American Indian	Asian	African-American	Hispanic	White
0.3	5	5	2	88

Thirty-three percent of higher education institutions experienced a net gain in minority faculty members from 1992–93 to 1993–94, 78 percent had no net change, and 5 percent had a net loss (*Chronicle* 1994, p. A44). If these trends continue, the disproportionate ratio of ethnic minority faculty members to minority students will worsen.

Minority Experiences and Background
Many problems minority students face in undergraduate and graduate education affect those students' career decisions. Research points to several difficulties:

1. *Since most minority college students are the first in their families to seek higher education, they are not knowledgeable about the work of the academy and the rules of its culture.*
2. *Minority students often feel alienated and unconnected at the university because they lack experience and contacts.*
3. *Since there is a dearth of successful minority . . . role models, most of the college students . . . will have white male mentors, if they are to have any at all* (Harris-Schenz 1990, p. 20).

Minority students are underrepresented in higher education for two reasons: (1) a general lack of sensitivity on the part of faculty, staff, and administrators; and (2) inadequate opportunities and support for minorities (Reed 1978; see also Leon 1993). These factors lead to decreased interest and motivation among minorities pursuing the professoriat. Moreover, the traditional framework for education functions as a barrier to access and equity at some institutions. The following practices, for example, deter minority faculty:

1. The hiring of underrepresented minorities only for certain specialized ethnic departments.
2. Limiting the number of minority faculty in mainstream departments.
3. Vague institutional hiring goals.

4. Inappropriate or limited advertising and recruitment for available faculty positions.
5. Playing women and minority candidates against each other in the competition for positions.
6. A lack of positive, equitable leadership in the administrative ranks.
7. Limited funding for affirmative action and equal opportunity offices on campuses.
8. Institutional inefficiency and ineptitude, and/or a lack of enforcement regarding compliance (see, e.g., Altbach and Lomotey 1991; Menges and Exum 1983).

Additionally, language, racial, and cultural barriers exist within the academic environment. And the notion of token minority faculty members has fueled and perpetuated the myth that minorities are not fully qualified for academic positions.

What's Different for Minority Faculty

Decisions and conditions surrounding minority faculty—including advising, service, tenure, and promotion—can be different from those experienced by majority faculty members. Minority colleagues tend to be "more burdened with service activities we advise other junior faculty colleagues to defer" (National Education Association 1991, p. 159). Minority colleagues may be "saddled with the dirty chores of the department and time-consuming committee appointments that may leave little time for research and scholarship" (Blackwell 1989, p. 13).

Other responsibilities and assignments are delegated to minority faculty members because the administration assumes that minorities, with their race or ethnic background or presumed knowledge of cultural differences, are best suited for specific tasks:

1. *Being called upon to be the expert on matters of diversity within the organization, even though [minority faculty members] may not be knowledgeable on the issues or very comfortable in the role;*
2. *Being called upon, often repeatedly, to educate individuals in the majority group about diversity, even though this is not part of the job description and [minority faculty members] are not given any authority or recognition to go along with the responsibility;*

Decisions and conditions surrounding minority faculty—including advising, service, tenure, and promotion—can be different from those experienced by majority faculty members.

3. *Serving on an affirmative action committee or task force that culminates in the rehashing of many of the same recommendations that [minority faculty members] have seen in the past with little real structural change ever taking place;*

4. *Serving as the liaison between the organization and the ethnic community, even though [minority faculty members] may not agree with the way the organization's policies impact on the community;*

5. *Taking time away from [minority faculty members'] own work to serve as general problem solver . . . for disagreements that arise in part because of sociocultural differences. . . ;*

6. *Being called upon to translate official documents . . . or to serve as interpreters . . .* (Padilla 1994, p. 26).

With regard to research and scholarship, minority faculty members are often subject to criticism when they conduct research using nonpositivistic research paradigms (Menges and Exum 1983) or pursue scholarly endeavors in areas or fields deemed less rigorous or academic (Garza 1993). Ethnic scholars' work is often subject to other common criticisms: (1) their scholarship is tangential and peripheral; (2) their research (perhaps conducted in the classroom, community, or clinical setting) was not research but service or teaching and thus not as valuable; and (3) their scholarship was not published in the "right" journals (Bronstein 1993).

In the experience of a minority faculty member seeking tenure:

> *A new sociology professor was interested in black ghetto kids' drug use. The rest of his department was more theoretically oriented and ideologically committed. He was not only sans a mentor, but odd man out. By going outside his department for support, he also alienated some of his colleagues. He did publish with a psychology member interested in criminal justice and finally developed a network of colleagues scattered about the U.S. He finally procured tenure after much hard work and support system building* (Cordova, Neely, and Shaughnessay 1988, p. 12).

Beyond the devaluing of research conducted by minorities, the issues arise of ambiguous college/university and departmental criteria and closed, confidential tenure and promotion decision making. Such decisions are "hairsplitting" practices that involve:

> . . . *making highly subjective and arbitrary judgment calls that frequently result in favor of whites over minorities. Many minority academics have not had opportunities to serve on faculty search committees. They have learned that final decisions are not as objective as minorities are led to believe. . . . Minorities, for example, are often not hired, promoted, or tenured—not for lack of required qualifications, but on the basis of paternalistic attitudes of the decision makers. . . . Hairsplitting practices are dangerous because they exclude [minorities] . . . from full incorporation into the academy simply on the basis of minor, subjective, and often inconsequential factors* (Reyes and Halcon 1991, pp. 176–77).

Other internal academic market factors limit the success of minority faculty in their quest for tenure and promotion: unclear, nonspecific job descriptions; vague, inconsistent, and irregular performance evaluations; lack of institutional information; distance from the social circles of the predominate faculty group, both in race and in rank; and lack of friendship and collegiality (Exum et al. 1984). As one African-American senior professor noted, "It is important to be liked, and probably at a much deeper political level than we are often aware of" (p. 318).

In 1989, full-time minority faculty members achieved the following tenure rates (*Department Chair* 1992):

African-American	61.0 percent
Hispanic	63.9 percent
Asian-American	59.8 percent
American Indian	66.6 percent

As of 1994, however, administrators from 508 private and public colleges and universities reported that the number of minority faculty members who had achieved tenure from 1992–93 to 1993–94 experienced a net gain at 18 percent of the institutions, no net change at 78 percent, and a net loss at 3 percent (*Chronicle* 1994, p. A44). To this day, the majority of tenured faculty members are white and male.

To address minority faculty members' concerns about tenure and promotion, professional organizations have begun to discuss alternatives for career faculty. Admittedly, the inflexibility of the present tenure system has created problems for postsecondary education. The American Association for Higher Education, for example, is conducting a two-year project to reexamine the traditional processes of tenure and to design more flexible career paths for professors. "If there are going to be limited opportunities, how are we going to accommodate minorities? There hasn't been any real growth in the proportion of tenured minority faculty. [And] the tenure quota system has contributed to that" (Magner 1995, p. A17).

The Research on Mentoring Minority Faculty

The body of literature on mentoring minority faculty is limited. One large study of scientists reports that minority academicians have difficulty gaining access to "eminent mentors whose sponsorship can help jump-start their careers," and "a series . . . of race-related difficulties [makes it difficult to sustain] mentoring relationships within the academic system" (Grant, Ward, and Forshner 1993, p. 25). This study also points to a pattern of accumulative disadvantages that keep minorities at the "outer circle" of their disciplines (p. 1).

Most studies of mentoring minority faculty are qualitative in nature, with a high concentration of essays, commentaries, and reflective pieces noting the importance of minorities as role models in education. The available research stresses that strategies need to be examined that would attract, retain, and advance African-Americans, Hispanics, Asians, and Native Americans within the educational system. Researchers have asserted that institutionally structured mentoring is a means of dispelling stereotypes, eliminating tokenism, and providing sustained support to minority professionals.

African-American faculty

The proportion of African-American faculty in higher education institutions has fluctuated from the 1960s to 1989, with no substantial growth evident. The representation of African-American faculty at predominantly white universities is poorer than at traditionally black institutions, and fewer

African-Americans are found in the ranks of associate and full professors (see, e.g., Mickelson and Oliver 1991).

Fewer African-American Ph.D.'s are in the academic pipeline. An assumption is sometimes made that if African-American candidates "are not trained in the graduate departments of universities considered to be the best in a field, it is concluded, often incorrectly, that no qualified black candidates are available" (Mickelson and Oliver 1991, p. 150). But the best African-American graduate students are not found only at the most elite, most prestigious institutions:

> *Because of family obligations, community ties, hostile social and racial climates on elite campuses, inadequate social and psychological support systems at leading schools, or limited financial support, well-qualified minority group members may enroll in a wide variety of schools rather than following the path that leads to elite universities* (Mickelson and Oliver 1991, pp. 161–62).

Only one out of five African-American students participates in mentoring relationships, and most African-Americans do not engage in mentoring in higher education (Blackwell 1989; see also Washington 1989). This statistic is further evidenced in professional mentoring experiences for African-American female faculty members. African-American faculty have the lowest faculty progression, retention, and tenure rates in academe, with African-American women having the least representation among tenured faculty; in fact, 22 percent of the female African-American educational professionals in one study did not have a mentor (Howard-Vital and Morgan 1993). Nearly all, however (96 percent), indicated that they would like to be a mentor to a junior colleague.

> *Mentoring is especially useful early in the development of a career with senior faculty members mentoring their junior colleagues. . . . To move up the academic ladder, one depends heavily on the support of departmental colleagues. Without this sponsorship, many women and members of minority groups need to develop alternative avenues of support, such as finding mentors in other*

departments or at other institutions (Association of American Colleges 1989, p. 16).

The problems of equity in professional growth for African-American faculty indicate that "the pool of black faculty has recently begun to show signs of stagnation and decline. This situation has resulted in a serious debate over causal explanations that have as their base either past discriminatory policies or demographic realities that are directly devoid of any racial intent" (Jackson 1991, p. 136). African-American faculty in traditionally black institutions believe that inadequate facilities, time for personal study, and opportunities to attend professional meetings; salaries; and red tape affect their employment (Jackson 1991; see also Talbert-Hersi 1993).

Asian, Asian-American, and Pacific Island faculty

A "model minority myth" surrounds Asian students and faculty members, a myth that postulates that Asians as a non-white group have "made it" in academe despite their long history of discrimination (Chan and Wang 1991). Even though an increasing number of colleges and universities have embraced diversity in the faculty, fewer Asians are available to fill current positions. As statistics show, Asian faculty members to this day constitute a minority in institutions of higher education; even fewer numbers are represented in the higher levels of administration or present in positions of executive leadership and decision making (see, e.g., Takaki 1989).

Asian faculty members encounter problems in academe similar to other minority faculty members.

When the faculty was relatively homogeneous, there were few challenges to the decisions based on supposedly purely meritocratic values. Institutional practices, such as confidentiality in the peer review process and barring junior faculty from certain kinds of decision making, shore up the power of the senior faculty, while power based on scholarly reputation gained as a result of research and publications further undergird their authority (Chan and Wang 1991, pp. 58–59).

Collegial power, however, has been granted to Asian faculty in the natural sciences, as these educators "find it slightly easier to participate in the day-to-day social interaction that accompanies academic work because scientific research routinely requires teamwork" (Chan and Wang 1991, p. 59). Accordingly, a notable number of Asian scientists and engineers are found in higher education institutions, although this same type of collegial power is less existent in the humanities and social sciences.

Asian minority faculty members are often not included in affirmative action programs at educational institutions; perhaps because Asians appear to be making more progress than other minority groups, they are excluded from institutional support (Sands, Parson, and Duane 1992). A study of Asian tenured and tenure-track faculty members found that 54.3 percent had been mentored in their careers (compared to 70 percent of the white faculty respondents) (Sands, Parson, and Duane 1992). The Asian respondents stated that advice, support, and feedback were the most meaningful aspects of mentoring, noting additionally that there was a "built-in concept of superior to inferior" in mentoring and that issues of exploitation; language, racial, and cultural barriers; and sexual tension and sexism were evident (p. 127).

Of those Asian faculty members who had mentored other faculty, their protégés were largely minority males who were assistant and associate professors. These mentors felt that shared research interests, personal compatibility, and a shared research methodology should guide mentoring relationships. Based on the research, Asian faculty members have not adopted the concept of mentoring to the same extent as white faculty (Sands, Parson, and Duane 1992), but Asian faculty who did not have a mentor believed that mentors would have been valuable to their careers.

Native American faculty

Native American students are often visibly absent from educational institutions; therefore, the opportunities for this minority group to earn academic credentials as faculty are limited. Reservation students are often the first in their families to attend college, and the separation from their parents, families, and friends removes their central form of guidance and support. Financial and emotional support to continue education is often missing in Native American families (Bowker 1993), and contemporary tribes "do not place the same degree of value on [the attainment of education]. . . . Not all Indian tribes share attitudes [about] education that reflect the attitudes of mainstream America" (Warner 1992, p. 66). Native Americans have additionally faced several barriers to higher education:

1. Administrators promulgate policies that increase dissatisfaction, thus creating one more barrier to the enrollment of American Indians.
2. Faculty members' misconceptions of ethnic students' abilities result in faculty believing that Native American students are intellectually inferior to nonethnic students.
3. Faculty members have little understanding of American Indian cultures.
4. Native Americans enter college at a later age and as nontraditional students.
5. There is a lack of faculty willing to mentor Native American students (Tate and Schwartz 1993).

Colleges and universities have instituted programs to increase Native American enrollments; to retain, graduate, and matriculate these students; and to prepare them for the workforce. Although Native American students seek opportunities in higher education, they do not want to be discriminated against by a college or university that does not value and accommodate their cultural differences. Institutions "need to strengthen their resolve to identify promising ethnic students and to develop mentoring strategies to ensure their training involvement . . . and [their] success" (Padilla 1994, p. 26).

Like other minority faculty members, Native Americans have had to juggle the competing demands of the academic environment, including the struggle to achieve the "intellectual respectability necessary to survive in the academic establishment" (Kidwell 1991, p. 23). While many Native American faculty members have been published and have received tenure, their numbers are still very small.

In a survey of the mentoring experiences of Native American faculty at a comprehensive university (Luna 1995), respondents stated that they had had no formal professional mentoring experiences. Their mentors had been tribal members or matriarchal family members. These faculty members expressed concern over the transition to academe from the reservation and stated that institutional barriers were prevalent in their undergraduate years. They additionally noted few, if any, Native American professional role models at their undergraduate and graduate institutions.

With regard to the lack of Native American mentoring experiences, it has been argued that mentoring needs to start early in the lives of Native American students.

> *We are recommending that faculty and administrators recognize that they must (1) find undergraduates to motivate for graduate schools; (2) groom and support graduate students to excel and to pursue postdoctoral opportunities; (3) encourage and enable junior faculty to produce first-rate research; and (4) recognize and develop senior faculty to become both role models and active leaders in governance and administrative structures. The pipeline approach depends on the movement of underrepresented faculty all along the career trajectory* (Justin, Freitag, and Parker, cited in Leon 1993, p. 15).

The chances of this change's happening are far greater if educational institutions adopt mentoring programs for minorities (Leon 1993).

Hispanic faculty

Many of the problems Hispanic youth face influence the opportunities and directions that Hispanics take in higher education. Latino students can be described in the following ways:

1. They are diverse in terms of spoken language, immigration status, class, and generational affiliation.
2. They most likely attended segregated educational settings.
3. They attended schools with dropout rates between 40 and 80 percent.
4. They scored below the national average on achievement examinations.
5. They attended indigent and highly populated schools.
6. They are more often represented in nonacademic courses or programs.
7. They have been educated by teachers who are not sensitive to their concerns or issues or qualified to meet their educational needs (Latino Commission 1992).

Several authors have noted inequalities fostered by academic institutions:

1. Recruitment into graduate schools, academic departments, colleges, and universities is based on traditional mechanisms and steeped in race, gender, and class biases (Sierra 1993).
2. Institutions often follow—consciously or unconsciously— the "one-minority-per-pot syndrome" (Reyes and Halcon 1991).
3. Institutions often relegate Hispanic faculty members to ethnically oriented programs, referred to the "barriorization" of Hispanics (Reyes and Halcon 1991).

Arturo Madried, former president of the National Chicano Council on Higher Education, says:

> *The reasons why many Chicanos and Puerto Ricans have been unable to obtain positions [in higher education] are various. . . . Far more usual are those [scholars] who have not been able to obtain a position because their area of research is the Chicano or Puerto Rican experience; because their degree is not from a prestigious department or university; because they did not understand that they had to acquire a mentor or a sponsor while in graduate school; or because of institutional resistance* (Leon 1993, p. 11).

With regard to tenure and promotion, research conducted by Hispanic faculty members is often devalued, as "brown-on-brown" research (research related to minority topics) has been seen as narrow in scope and lacking objectivity (see, e.g., Garza 1993; Reyes and Halcon 1991). Moreover, Hispanic faculty assert that majority faculty may be unqualified to evaluate their research. Other responsibilities could negatively affect the tenure and promotion rates of Hispanic faculty: (1) heavy teaching and advising loads, (2) expected participation in minority-related committees, (3) demands by Hispanic communities, and (4) multiple requests from ethnic university students (Garza 1993).

Successful mentoring programs for Hispanic faculty need to consider basic cultural values, including:

1. *Allocentrism:* An emphasis on the needs, objectives, and points of view of the "in-group." Mentoring relationships provide a good fit with the value of allocentrism when mentors make explicit efforts to seek friendly interactions.
2. *Simpatia:* An emphasis on the need for behaviors that promote comfortable social relationships. A need exists for mentors to establish positive relationships with protégés.
3. *Familialism:* An emphasis on individuals' strong solidarity with nuclear and extended families. Mentors need to understand and respect this value and note obligations and support by the protégé's family.
4. *Power distance:* An emphasis on interpersonal power or influence that exists between two individuals. Mentors need to be aware of this value when communicating both verbally and nonverbally, noting that "power" may come from inherent traits (e.g., intelligence) or from inherited or acquired characteristics (e.g., money, education, position).
5. *Time orientation:* An emphasis on differences in terms of temporal orientation—that is, more flexible attitudes to- ward time than whites. The mentor needs to understand this value in terms of appointments, interviews, and so on.
6. *Gender roles:* An emphasis on gender-related behaviors for both sexes. Mentors may need to seek the trust and approval of those associated with the protégé.
7. *Personal space:* An emphasis on specific preferences in terms of the amount of physical space considered appro- priate between people. Mentors need to honor this value because differences in personal space affect the emotional reactions of protégés who interact with other individuals (Rosado 1994).

Same-Race Mentoring
Although the research is limited on same-race mentoring relationships in both community colleges and universities, same-race mentors offer the following benefits: (1) they seek to discover their similarities rather than focus on differences; and (2) they exhibit cultural sensitivity. Some research has shown that cross-race mentoring relationships have not been successful because of personal and organizational barriers (see, e.g., Collins 1982; Stenberg 1990; Stewart 1990).

Considerations for Minority Faculty

Mentoring programs and relationships for minority faculty should consider the following suggestions:

1. Pair minority faculty who need to build their research and scholarship with senior scholars.
2. Develop parameters for the relationship and include goals that address the nontraditional protégé's concerns.
3. Do not assume that minority faculty know the "rules of the game."
4. Exhibit cultural sensitivity and work to learn about the backgrounds of minority faculty.

Information on minority faculty members and mentoring is scarce. A policy of creating a mentoring program for all new and junior faculty of color should be encouraged. Within a mentoring program, higher education colleagues need to increase their involvement in ensuring that minority faculty receive departmental, college, and institutional support. Such involvement in turn renews and redirects the talents and interests of senior faculty mentors.

THE APPLICATION OF MENTORING

The art and skill of mentoring is often contingent on the institution's "common sense" and the functions it serves. Although every organization has its own culture, some general guidelines apply to successful faculty mentoring:

1. Mentoring needs to become an institutional practice, which requires a college or university to not only encourage mentoring but also support it formally with resources and through policy.
2. Mentoring needs to include plans for implementation and evaluation, which encompasses strategies for establishment of a mentoring program, commitment for continuation, and responsibility to monitor, improve, and enhance the program.
3. Mentoring needs to be supported by the faculty, which involves communication of the benefits of mentoring to the protégé, mentor, and institution, as well as the faculty's involvement in the creation, direction, and continuation of a mentoring program.

The art and skill of mentoring is often contingent on the institution's "common sense" and the functions it serves.

The following specific recommendations are also appropriate for mentoring in educational environments:

1. Include administrators and governing board members in the mentoring process.
2. Disseminate information about mentoring through campus newsletters and at faculty meetings.
3. Establish mentoring training programs for mentors and protégés.
4. Include mentoring activities in faculty performance evaluations.
5. Encourage faculty research on mentoring.
6. Offer recognition and/or financial incentives for participation in mentoring activities and programs (Association of American Colleges 1983).

With guidelines and recommendations taken into consideration, mentoring programs in education can still encounter barriers—campus politics, faculty unions and professional organizations, and the confidentiality of records and decisions related to faculty, technology, governance, and shrinking resources, for example. Research is limited on such barriers and concerns, although those interested in faculty mentoring programs will likely require this type of information.

The Myths of Mentoring

Although the literature on mentoring points out a multitude of benefits to the protégé, the mentor, and the organization, mentoring is not a panacea for all problems in a department, college, or institution. In fact, a field-based research project funded by the Women's Education Equity Act under the purview of the U.S. Department of Education has identified some myths of mentoring:

> **Myth 1:** *Mentoring is a reward in and of itself.* It is a myth that the mentoring process is inherently rewarding and that remuneration is therefore not necessary. While mentors do realize the benefits and "warm fuzzies" of teaching a protégé the ropes, the truth is that organizations need to reward those individuals who agree to take on additional responsibilities. Providing incentives turns mentoring into an important activity and a priority in the workplace.
>
> **Myth 2:** *Mentoring programs are a panacea for difficult problems, such as orientation, affirmative action, and problem employees.* Mentoring should be reserved for developing human potential in terms of improving organizational goals. Too frequently, quick-fix programs are initiated under the rubric of mentoring. Although the organization's problems need to be addressed, people should not confuse the programs to fix them with mentoring.
>
> **Myth 3:** *Any mentor and protégé can be paired.* Too often, mentors and protégés are thrown together with the assumption that a common workplace will be enough to make the relationship work. Sometimes a similar manner or personality is perceived to be an adequate link. If either the mentor or protégé is unwilling to participate or if one is uncomfortable within the pair, the relationship could be doomed. Not everyone is a good mentor or protégé, and participants' readiness, communication, volunteerism, compatibility, and mentoring style should be assessed. Carefully talking with the mentoring pair helps to ensure a better understanding of the relationship's potential viability.

Myth 4: *Mentoring programs must be controlled to be successful.* Organizations are known for operating policies and procedures, and this same philosophy is applied— mistakenly—to mentoring programs. Each member of the pair has different needs and developmental considerations. Training and guidelines are important, but a successful mentoring program allows individualized goals jointly drawn from the pair. Organizations benefit when they provide resources for the pair and do not hamper their progress (Mertz, Welch, and Henderson 1990).

Other considerations in mentoring programs should include communications and information. Academic institutions cannot assume that personnel have the same understanding of and perceptions about mentoring. Knowledge about mentoring can vary based on individual mentoring experiences or the lack thereof. Nor can colleges and universities assume that mentoring will be accepted within the faculty and/or administrative ranks. Mentoring programs can be met with skepticism or resistance from the organization's members who want to maintain the status quo. Further, mentoring could intimidate people, threaten turf, or increase departmental politicking.

It is also important to remember that mentoring might not automatically change institutional expectations, solve a disappointing career situation, remedy a career that has reached a plateau, reduce stagnation and withdrawal of individual faculty members, change attitudes, or build requisite personal and professional skills. Moreover, mentoring might not be viewed positively, and it could indeed be perceived as a form of tokenism or favoritism.

The myth exists that the mentor always knows best, but "mentors are human like the rest of us and may make mistakes or deliberately [or inadvertently] exploit the protégé" (Sandler 1993, p. B3). This situation could include misperception of the protégé's potential and/or goals and the pursuit of a mentor's personal agenda. "The mentor must see benefit in contributing to another person's development and must be at a [career] stage . . . where collegial development is a high priority" (Campbell 1992, p. 78).

The Virtues of Mentoring
Research on mentoring has clearly identified qualifications of mentors in successful mentoring relationships. These qualifica-

tions fall within categories of personal and professional skills, knowledge, and attitudes. Some misconceptions have arisen that one hierarchical relationship will embody the needs of a protégé and be reciprocal for the mentor, but mentors might not possess a full range of qualifications required to meet all of the protégé's needs. A singular mentoring relationship might not be sufficient within a faculty member's professional career. Faculty might need to use multiple mentors, for example, relationship constellations and external mentors.

Kram's seminal work on mentoring in the workplace stresses mentoring as a developmental process that evolves throughout one's profession, addressing career stages, an organization's concern for employees' productivity, and the quality of the work environment (1986). Mentoring relationships need to be addressed over one's adult life so that "individuals . . . consciously identify the kinds of developmental alliances that are critical at a given time . . . and enable organizations to create avenues for employees to build such relationships" (p. 173).

Qualifications of a mentor
Researchers on mentoring agree that successful mentors possess certain qualifications, and although these characteristics can be classified in a variety of ways, they tend to be integrated personal and professional virtues that enrich a mentoring relationship for both the protégé and the mentor.

Personal attributes include honesty, reliability, mutual caring, sharing, giving, patience, and strong interpersonal skills (see, e.g., Kram 1986). Desirable professional qualities consist of knowledge of the organization and its experiences, technical and disciplinary competence, professional influence and status, willingness to promote another's professional growth, and knowledge about how to advance in a career (see, e.g., Murray 1991).

Certain specific questions help to identify mentors within educational organizations:

1. *What is the mentor's own achievement in key areas?*
2. *What is the mentor's relationship to various groups and networks in the department, institution, and discipline?*
3. *Is the mentor someone who believes whole-heartedly in [the protégé's] abilities?*
4. *What has happened to the [mentor's] former mentees?*

5. *Is the mentor not only good at giving advice and direction, but also able to understand [the protégé's] own views about [his or her] needs and goals?* (Association of American Colleges 1983, p. 6).

Each mentoring relationship is different, depending on the protégé's and the mentor's needs and departmental and institutional goals and circumstances. It is important that faculty protégés examine mentoring possibilities and make critical inquiries that can affect the success of mentoring relationships in the academic arena.

Qualifications of a protégé

The question of whether everyone should become a protégé is still being studied in education and in business and industry. Although certain characteristics of good mentors have been associated with successful mentoring relationships, distinguishing qualifications of potential protégés are less clear. Research has focused on succession-planning techniques to identify protégé target groups and diagnose a protégé's developmental needs.

The goal of determining faculty protégés who will benefit from mentoring relationships includes the processes of self-nomination, nomination by a supervisor, and nomination by a sponsor. Self-nomination can be made by any person who wishes to participate in a mentoring program. Nomination by a supervisor requires the submission of potential protégés' names from those who know of their potential to grow and develop additional skills. And nomination by a sponsor involves recommending a protégé based on experience with the assessment of the candidate's potential, whether the sponsor is in a direct supervisory role or not (Murray 1991, pp. 118–21).

Business and industry have used formal, external diagnostic tools to ascertain employees' developmental needs, including pen-and-pencil tests, self-evaluations, lifestyle inventories, assessment of leadership skills, simulations, and in-basket exercises. Because of the varying stages of a faculty member's career, however, diagnosing individual faculty needs and goals is more complex.

An ideal protégé is a person who is goal oriented, is willing to assume responsibility for his or her own growth, seeks challenging assignments and greater responsibility, and is receptive to feedback and coaching (Rooney, Ida, Nolt, and Adhern, cited in Murray 1991, p. 123). Faculty protégés also need to identify their professional needs, assist in the development of activities to accomplish those needs, maintain a commitment to the mentoring relationship, and be realistic and flexible about the outcomes of mentoring and the time and resources required.

Protégés need to realize that mentoring requires more than a technical matching of protégé and mentor. Protégés should realize that while protégés can benefit from people they respect professionally but do not like personally, fostering relationships with people whom they both respect and like will enhance the likelihood of successful mentoring (Clawson and Blank, cited in Murray 1991, p. 13).

A Model for Planned Mentoring

Generic components are necessary for success in planned mentoring (Gray 1989b). Before implementation, the purposes and goals of mentoring should be examined for compatibility with the organization's development, policies, and culture. Consider, for example, whether planned mentoring would be compatible with affirmative action for female faculty. During implementation of the program, participants are identified and matched, trained, monitored, and evaluated (see figure 2). A practical approach to a planned program would include the following considerations:

1. A developmental approach would ensure congruence between the mentoring program's goals and objectives and those of the organization.
2. Voluntary participation and strong administrative support are musts.
3. Mentoring is a developmental approach for the long haul. Mentoring should not be used as a band-aid for an organization's problems.
4. The desired goals, benefits, and outcomes of mentoring must be predetermined. Once they are identified, selecting participants and planning the training will fall into place.
5. Start with a small pilot program for a short time period (six to 12 months recommended). After its evaluation, implement those suggestions that strengthen the objectives, process, and outcomes.

6. Orientation for participants should be complete to ensure their buying into the program. It should include detailed information about such components as time necessary, duration, type of training provided, frequency of interaction, and verifiable outcomes.
7. Select volunteer mentors and protégés carefully to enhance the achievement of goals and outcomes.
8. Unsuccessful mentoring is a result of little or no training for participants. Mentors need to learn what is expected and how to provide the best interaction.
9. Monitoring the personal interactions in the mentoring relationship is necessary and may prevent emerging problems. Training, although necessary, will not automatically prevent problems.
10. Measure the progress of the program's goals and outcomes. Evaluation and feedback only enhance success (Gray 1989b).

FIGURE 2

PLANNED MENTORING CYCLE

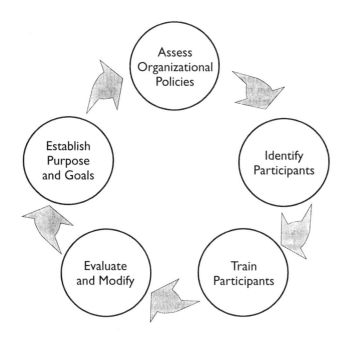

Activities and interaction between members of a mentoring dyad can be facilitated through the suggestions outlined in table 7 to help participants become oriented to career development and personal interactions. Many guides are available to assist individuals and organizations with those first but careful steps.

TABLE 7

**GETTING STARTED: ACTIVITIES FOR
PLANNED MENTORING**

1. Share the highs and lows of a career path by telling a personal story.

2. Invite VIPs and other leaders to share their career stories and mentoring experiences.

3. Have protégés complete a self-assessment of competency in their disciplines and discuss the outcomes.

4. Allow the mentor to select a reading (a book or article, for example) related to the goals of the program. Report on the reading and discuss it with other mentoring pairs.

5. Develop short- and long-range career development plans.

6. Find ways to work on projects together—at least temporarily.

7. Arrange for protégés to visit and/or visualize various components of the organization.

8. Take protégés to formal and informal management meetings. Debrief the protégé later about those events.

Source: Phillips-Jones 1983.

Faculty Mentoring Models

The Academic Council at Sinclair Community College formed the Mentor Committee in 1978 to provide a mechanism for developing qualified and highly effective part-time instructors (Hosey, Carranza, White, and Kaur 1990). The goals of the program are to maintain instructional support, improve coordination and professional relationships between part- and full-time faculty, and provide opportunities to develop instructional or administrative skills of full-time faculty.

The committee published clear and definitive steps to achieve these outcomes. A job description for mentors and policies for selection and remuneration were decided, and after protégés are selected, they are assigned to mentors in their departments. Tips and activities are listed to facilitate the program's goals. The primary activities are orientation to campus support services and departmental/college policies. Classroom observation is required, with the means for feedback and coaching to enhance learning. Protégés and mentors alike complete evaluation forms to assist in continued improvement of the program.

In a peer mentoring program at a community college, pairs developed individualized objectives, activities, methods, and evaluations (Harnish and Wild 1993). Mentoring centered around team teaching, test development, technological instruction, and learning across the curriculum. In one instance, a senior faculty mentor assisted her junior colleague in updating specific nursing skills, with the goal to improve the effectiveness of clinical and laboratory instruction for students. This mentoring strategy was effective in remedying problem areas and weaknesses of the faculty protégé. Both the mentor and the protégé worked toward program goals. The program had strong support from the administration, and stipends or reduced workloads were offered as incentives to participate in the program.

In a research mentoring program for a discipline-specific profession, a workshop with individualized mentoring goals focused on advancing the protégé toward a funded project (Wofford, Boysen, and Riding 1991). Mentors assisted protégés to learn skills of clearly communicating the scope of the study and defining researchable questions. A five-year evaluation was carried out to determine achievements in interaction and funding.

Highlights of the Models
Mentoring is best used for specific purposes and goals and with faculty who volunteer to participate. Process, philosophy, expectations, and remuneration should be incorporated into the educational institution's framework and structure. Mentoring must not be approached haphazardly, with mismatched pairs or with restrictive administrative control. Mentors must be qualified for the identified program and be willing to share their knowledge and power. Protégés must be open to feedback, constructive criticism, and changes to thinking, behavior, and attitudes. With commitment to the mentoring relationship, progress and growth will occur.

A stepwise approach to facilitated mentoring works. Mentoring programs generally have similar steps, but each purpose, activity, and outcome is customized to better fit institutional and/or individual requirements. Mentoring remains a significant and empowering strategy for faculty throughout their careers.

Because most faculty mentoring programs are relatively new, few evaluative studies have been conducted. More research is necessary in this area.

CONCLUSIONS AND RECOMMENDATIONS

If mentoring is to succeed in academe, it must be supported by all sectors, implying that faculty, potential protégés and mentors, administrators, presidents, and governing boards alike must integrate a philosophy of mentoring into the organization's culture. Mentoring must be valued as a means to emphasize, support, and empower human resources.

Mentoring can be a tool or a philosophical framework used for a variety of reasons. Mentoring junior colleagues in teaching and scholarship and mentoring faculty for leadership roles are important agenda items for institutions. Moreover, the promotion of women and faculty of color in the professoriat is critical. Mentoring enhances productivity, addresses collegiality, and could do more to recruit, retain, and advance faculty.

Models of mentoring and research from business strongly support the need for mentoring in organizations. Mentoring strengthens the organization and supports the institution's vision, and organizations with mentoring programs exhibit increased effectiveness and collaboration (Murray 1991).

Faculty career development, better teaching, quality research, and improved leadership skills can be positive outcomes of mentoring. A single mentor or multiple peer mentors have a significant effect on faculty's productivity and growth. Most difficult for faculty new to an institution is the understanding of internal politics. Mentoring empowers faculty in that they are able to analyze and formulate solutions to complex problems.

Mentoring is an age-old concept that promotes human development. Through this concept, individuals can more fully experience and realize their potential. In a predictable cyclical fashion, the protégé becomes mentor to a new generation. Special challenges and opportunities are important for women and minorities, and mentoring in the academic environment should be customized to the career development of particular faculty members. For example, needs of novice female faculty members are likely different from those of midcareer faculty. As a priority, mentoring should advance individuals' professional and personal goals. In the end, the organization can improve.

Mentoring is an excellent framework that can assist in transforming the academic environment while enhancing the faculty's potential (Caldwell and Carter 1993, pp. 213–19). As such, the following recommendations should be noted:

Faculty career development, better teaching, quality research, and improved leadership skills can be positive outcomes of mentoring.

1. Mentoring is effective in the learning organization. Each part of the organization must be open to change and learn new ways when necessary. Orders from the top down by one learned leader are no longer effective during a time when quality or continuous improvement management is operational and the goal is faculty growth.
2. Mentoring may be effective for restructuring the academic workplace. Restructuring, reengineering, and "right-sizing" are all means of transforming the organizational structure to achieve the most comprehensive human resource benefits. In the academy, the process might mean shifting departments or changing the academic mission. Because mentoring can focus on the promotion of organizational goals, its potential should be examined.
3. Mentoring is best viewed as one of many ways to assist a faculty member in complex roles as "teacher" and "researcher." It should *not* be the only method of promoting effectiveness or developing potential.
4. Mentoring and mentoring programs should be implemented within the larger context of the college or university. Mentoring programs should complement the mission and goals of the institution.
5. Training mentors and time for mentoring activities are necessary to help move mentoring forward. Lip service is not enough. Resources must be dedicated to mentoring efforts. To realize appropriate outcomes and changes in the academic environment, a focus on the purpose and dedication to resources is necessary: otherwise, efforts are fruitless.
6. Various mentoring programs and designs are possible, and institutions should consider manageable activities and goals when designing mentoring programs. All outcomes should be measurable, and progress should be monitored.
7. Institutions should avoid forced recruiting of mentors and protégés but *encourage* participation in mentoring activities. Voluntary mentoring programs are preferable, because individuals have noted their interest, but such programs do not preclude paying participants.
8. Education should be prepared for potential challenges. Any mentoring activity will always include a few problems and barriers, but continuous monitoring and solicita-

tion of ideas and recommendations from faculty will help to ameliorate them.

Mentoring is a lifelong effort and process. Each of us has the potential to mentor another individual and to promote the role model of mentor to our colleagues. Moreover, mentoring is a powerful institutional strategy for personalizing individual faculty development. Most important, mentoring is a philosophy about people and how critical they are to an organization.

FACULTY MENTORING PROGRAMS

The following educational institutions have formalized faculty mentoring programs as of 1995. It is not a comprehensive list. Many other community colleges and universities have excellent programs.

Arizona Western College, Yuma, Arizona
Austin Community College, Austin, Texas
California State University, Los Angeles, California
Eastern Michigan University, Ypsilanti, Michigan
Florida Community College, Jacksonville, Florida
Indiana University, Indianapolis, Indiana
Los Medanos College, Pittsburg, California
National University, San Diego and Irvine, California
Palm Beach Atlantic College, West Palm Beach, Florida
Pima Community College, Tucson, Arizona
Pittsburg State University, Pittsburg, Kansas
Purdue University, West Lafayette, Indiana
Southern Illinois University, Carbondale, Illinois
University of Albany, Albany, New York
University of Alberta, Edmonton, Alberta, Canada
University of Georgia, Athens, Georgia
Western Carolina University, Cullowhee, North Carolina

REFERENCES

The Educational Resources Information Center (ERIC) Clearinghouse on Higher Education abstracts and indexes the current
literature on higher education for inclusion in ERIC's database and
announcement in ERIC's monthly bibliographic journal, *Resources
in Education* (RIE). Most of these publications are available
through the ERIC Document Reproduction Service (EDRS). For
publications cited in this bibliography that are available from EDRS,
ordering number and price code are included. Readers who wish
to order a publication should write to the ERIC Document Reproduction Service, 3900 Wheeler Avenue, Alexandria, Virginia
22304. (Phone orders with VISA or MasterCard are taken at
800/227-ERIC or 703/823-0500.) When ordering, please specify the
document (ED) number. Documents are available as noted in
microfiche (MF) and paper copy (PC). If you have the price code
ready when you call EDRS, an exact price can be quoted. The last
page of the latest issue of *Resources in Education* also has the
current cost, listed by code.

Altbach, P.G., and K. Lomotey, eds. 1991. *The Racial Crisis in
American Higher Education.* Albany: State Univ. of New York
Press.

American Association of Colleges for Teacher Education. 1992.
"Induction and Mentoring." *Journal of Teacher Education* 43(3):
163–226.

Association of American Colleges. 1983. "Academic Mentoring for
Women Students and Faculty: A New Look at an Old Way to Get
Ahead." Washington, D.C.: Project on the Status and Education
of Women. ED 240 891. 17 pp. MF–01; PC–01.

———. 1986. *The Campus Climate Revisited: Chilly for Women
Faculty, Administrators, and Graduate Students.* Washington,
D.C.: Project on the Status and Education of Women. ED 298
837. 112 pp. MF–01; PC–05.

———. 1989. *Black Women in Academe: Issues and Strategies.*
Washington, D.C.: Project on the Status and Education of
Women. ED 311 817. 29 pp. MF–01; PC–02.

Astin, H.S., and C. Leland. 1991. *Women of Influence, Women of
Vision: A Cross-generational Study of Leaders and Social
Change.* San Francisco: Jossey-Bass.

Ballantine, J.H. 1989. *Schools and Society.* Mountain View, Calif.:
Mayfield Publishing Co.

Bardwick, J.M. 1980. "The Seasons of a Woman's Life." In *Women's
Lives: New Theory, Research, and Policy,* edited by D.G. Mc-
Guigan. Ann Arbor: Univ. of Michigan Press.

Barowsky, D. September/October 1988. "Women's Networks Mean Business." *Healthcare Executive:* 36–38.

Beer, M. 1980. *Organizational Change and Development: A System View.* Santa Monica, Calif.: Goodyear Publishing.

Bergen, D., and J. Connelly. 1988. "The Collegial Research Mentor Project: A Model for Faculty Research and Scholarship Development." *International Journal of Mentoring* 2(1): 3–8.

Blackburn, R.T., D.W. Chapman, and S.M. Cameron. 1981. "Cloning in Academe: Mentorship and Academic Careers." *Research in Higher Education* 15(4): 315–27.

Blackwell, J.E. 1989. "Mentoring: An Action Strategy for Increasing Minority Faculty." *Academe* 78: 8–14.

Bogat, G., and R. Redner. 1985. "How Mentoring Affects the Professional Development of Women in Psychology." *Professional Psychology: Research and Practice* 16: 851–59.

Boice, R. 1992. "Lessons Learned about Mentoring." In *Developing New and Junior Faculty,* edited by M.D. Sorcinelli and A.E. Austin. San Francisco: Jossey-Bass.

Bolton, E.B. 1980. "A Conceptual Analysis of the Mentor Relationship in the Career Development of Women." *Adult Education* 30(4): 195–207.

Bowker, A. 1993. *Sisters in the Blood: The Education of Women in Native America.* Newton, Mass.: WEEA Publishing Center.

Bronstein, P. 1993. "Challenges, Rewards, and Costs for Feminist and Ethnic Minority Scholars." In *Building a Diverse Faculty,* edited by J. Gainen and R. Boice. San Francisco: Jossey-Bass.

Burack, E.H. April 1984. "The Sphinx's Riddle: Life and Career Cycles." *Training and Development Journal:* 52–61.

Bureau of Labor Statistics. May 1992. *Occupational Projections and Training Data, 1992 Edition: A Statistical and Research Supplement to the 1992–93 Occupational Outlook Handbook.* Bulletin 2401. Washington, D.C.: U.S. Dept. of Labor.

Busch, J.W. 1983. "An Analysis of Mentoring Relationships in Schools of Education." Ph.D. dissertation, Univ. of New Mexico.

Caldwell, B.J., and E. Carter, eds. 1993. *The Return of the Mentor: Strategies for Workplace Learning.* Washington, D.C.: Falmer Press.

Cameron, S.W., and R.T. Blackburn. 1981. "Sponsorship and Academic Career Success." *Journal of Higher Education* 52(4): 369–77.

Campbell, W.H. 1992. "Mentoring of Junior Faculty." *American Journal of Pharmaceutical Education* 56(1): 75–79.

Carlson, R. 1972. "Understanding Women: Implications for

Personality Theory and Research." *Journal of Social Issues* 28(2): 17–32.

Carnegie Foundation for the Advancement of Teaching. 1989. *The Condition of the Professorate*. Princeton, N.J.: Author. ED 312 963. 162 pp. MF–01; PC not available EDRS.

Carter, H.M. 1982. "Making It in Academia: Gurus Can Get You There." Paper presented at an annual meeting of the American Educational Research Association, April, New York, New York. ED 235 758. 19 pp. MF–01; PC not available EDRS.

Chalmers, R.K. 1992. "Faculty Development: The Nature and Benefits of Mentoring." *American Journal of Pharmaceutical Education* 56(1): 71–74.

Chan, S., and L. Wang. 1991. "Racism and the Model Minority: Asian-Americans in Higher Education." In *The Racial Crisis in American Higher Education,* edited by P.G. Altbach and K. Lomotey. Albany: State Univ. of New York Press.

Chao, G.T, P.M. Walz, and P.D. Gardner. 1992. "Formal and Informal Mentorships: A Comparison on Mentoring Functions and Contrast with Nonmentored Counterparts." *Personnel Psychology* 45: 619–36.

Chronicle of Higher Education. 16 September 1992. "Notes" 39(4): A7.

———. 1 September 1994. "Almanac" 51(1): A18+.

———. 28 April 1995. "Trends Affecting Affirmative Action" 41(33): A33.

Clark, S.M., and M. Corcoran. 1986. "Perspectives on the Professional Socialization of Women Faculty." *Journal of Higher Education* 57(1): 20–43.

Clawson, J.G., and M.B. Blank. 1990. "What Really Counts in Superior-Subordinate Relationships? Lessons from Business." *Mentoring International* 4(1): 12–16.

Collins, G.C., and P. Scott. 1979. "Everyone Who Makes It Has a Mentor." *Harvard Business Review* 56(1): 89–101.

Collins, R. 1982. "Colonialism on Campus: A Critique of Mentoring to Achieve Equity in Higher Education." Paper presented at an annual meeting of the American Educational Research Association, April, New York, New York. ED 235 760. 17 pp. MF–01; PC not available EDRS.

Commission on the Status of Women. 1990. *Reaching the Vision: Women in Arizona's Universities in the Year 2000*. Phoenix: Arizona Board of Regents.

Cordova, F., R. Neely, and M.F. Shaughnessay. 1988. "Mentoring Women and Minorities in Higher Education." Portales: Eastern

New Mexico Univ., Psychology Department. ED 325 005. 19 pp. MF–01; PC–01.

Cullen, D.L., and G. Luna. 1993. "Women Mentoring in Academe: Addressing the Gender Gap in Higher Education." *Gender and Education* 5(2): 125–37.

Daloz, L.A. 1986. *Effective Teaching and Mentoring*. San Francisco: Jossey-Bass.

Dalton, G., P. Thompson, and R. Price. 1977. "The Four Stages of Professional Careers." *Organizational Dynamics* 6: 22–23.

The Department Chair. Summer 1992. "Full-time Faculty Tenure Rates by Race/Ethnicity and Sex, Selected Years" 3(1): 16.

Diehl, P.F., and R. Simpson. 1989. "Investing in Junior Faculty: The Teaching Improvement Program." *Innovative Higher Education* 13(2): 147–57.

Dreher, G.F., and R.A. Ash. 1990. "A Comparative Study of Mentoring among Men and Women in Managerial, Professional, and Technical Positions." *Journal of Applied Psychology* 76(5): 539–46.

Erikson, E.H. 1963. *Childhood and Society*. 2d ed. New York: W.W. Norton.

———, ed. 1978. *Adulthood*. New York: W.W. Norton.

Exum, W.H., R.M. Menges, B. Watkins, and P. Berglund. 1984. "Making It at the Top: Women and Minority Faculty in the Academic Labor Market." *American Behavioral Scientist* 27: 301–24.

Fagenson, E.A. 1989. "The Mentor Advantage: Perceived Career/Job Experiences of Protégés versus Nonprotégés." *Journal of Organizational Behavior* 10: 309–20.

Faver, C.A. 1980. "Generational and Life-cycle Effects on Women's Achievement Orientation." In *Women's Lives: New Theory, Research, and Policy,* edited by D.G. McGuigan. Ann Arbor: Univ. of Michigan Press.

Galvez-Hjornevik, C. 1985. "Teacher Mentors: A Review of the Literature." Ph.D. dissertation, Univ. of Texas at Austin.

Garza, H. 1993. "Second-class Academics: Chicano/Latino Faculty in U.S. Universities." In *Building a Diverse Faculty,* edited by J. Gainen and R. Boice. San Francisco: Jossey-Bass.

Gilbert, L.A., and K.M. Rossman. 1992. "Gender and the Mentoring Process for Women: Implications for Professional Development." *Professional Psychology: Research and Practice* 23(3): 233–38.

Gilligan, C. 1982. *In a Different Voice*. Cambridge, Mass.: Harvard Univ. Press.

Grant, L., K.B. Ward, and C. Forshner. 1993. "Mentoring, Gender, and Careers of Academic Scientists." Paper presented at an annual meeting of the American Educational Research Association, April, Atlanta, Georgia. ED 361 299. 40 pp. MF–01; PC not available EDRS.

Gray, W.A. 1989a. "Advice on Planning Mentoring Programs for At-Risk Youth." *Mentoring International* 3(3): 17–22.

———. 1989b. "Situational Mentoring: Custom Designing Planned Mentoring Programs." *Mentoring International* 3(1): 19–28.

Hanson, P.A. 1983. "Protégé Perceptions of the Mentor-Protégé Relationship: Its Complementary Nature and Developmental Tasks." Ph.D. dissertation, Univ. of Wisconsin.

Harnish, D., and L.A. Wild. 1993. "Faculty Peer Mentoring: A Strategy for Improving Instruction." *Community College Journal* 64(1): 22–27.

Harris-Schenz, B. 1990. "Helping with the Bootstraps: The Mentor's Task." *ADFL Bulletin* 21(3): 18–21.

Harvard Educational Review. 1981. "On Generativity and Identity: From a Conversation with Erik and Joan Erikson" 512: 249–69.

Healy, C.C., and A.J. Welchert. 1990. "Mentoring Relationships: A Definition to Advance Research and Practice." *Educational Researcher* 19(9): 17–21.

Hennig, M., and A. Jardim. 1977. *The Managerial Woman.* Garden City, N.Y.: Anchor/Doubleday.

Hosey, P., Y. Carranza, M. White, and H. Kaur. 1990. *A Guide to Mentoring.* 3d rev. ed. Dayton: Sinclair Community College.

Howard-Vital, M., and R. Morgan. 1993. "African-American Women and Mentoring." Edinboro, Pa.: Edinboro Univ. ED 360 425. 13 pp. MF–01; PC–01.

Ilgen, D.R., and M.A. Youtz. 1986. "Factors Affecting the Evaluation and Development of Minorities in Organizations." *Research in Personnel and Human Resources Management:* 307–37.

Jackson, K.W. 1991. "Black Faculty in Academia." In *The Racial Crisis in American Higher Education,* edited by P.G. Altbach and K. Lomotey. Albany: State Univ. of New York Press.

Jarvis, D.K. 1992. "Improving Junior Faculty Scholarship." In *Developing New and Junior Faculty,* edited by M.D. Sorcinelli and A.E. Austin. San Francisco: Jossey-Bass.

Johnsrud, L., and M. Wunsch. 1991. "Barriers to Success in Academic Life: Perceptions of Faculty Women in a Colleague Pairing Program." Paper presented at an annual meeting of the Association for the Study of Higher Education, October 31–November 3, Boston, Massachusetts.

Josefowitz, N. 1982. *Paths to Power.* Reading, Mass.: Addison-Wesley.

Kanter, R.M. 1977. *Men and Women of the Corporation*. New York: Basic Books.

Katz, P.A. 1979. "The Development of Female Identity." *Sex Roles* 5(2): 155–78.

Kidwell, C.S. 1991. "The Vanishing Native Reappears in the College Curriculum." *Change* 23(2): 19–26.

Knox, P.L., and T.V. McGovern. 1988. "Mentoring Women in Academia." *Teaching of Psychology* 15(1): 39–41.

Korn/Ferry International and John E. Anderson Graduate School of Management, UCLA. 1990. *Korn/Ferry International's Executive Profile 1990: A Survey of Corporate Leaders*. New York: Korn/Ferry International.

Kram, K.E. 1983. "Phases of the Mentor Relationship." *Academy of Management Journal* 26(4): 608–25.

———. 1985. *Mentoring at Work: Developmental Relationships in Organization Life*. Glenview, Ill.: Scott, Foresman.

———. 1986. "Mentoring in the Workplace." In *Career Development in Organizations,* edited by D.T. Hall. San Francisco: Jossey-Bass.

Kram, K.E., and L.A. Isabella. 1985. "Mentoring Alternatives: The Role of Peer Relationships in Career Development." *Academy of Management Journal* 28(1): 110–32.

Latino Commission on Educational Reform. 1992. *Toward a Vision for the Education of Latino Students*. New York: Author.

Leatherman, C. 21 April 1995. "Outpacing Inflation." *Chronicle of Higher Education* 41(32): A16.

Leon, D.J. 1993. *Mentoring Minorities in Higher Education: Passing the Torch*. Washington, D.C.: National Education Association, Office of Higher Education. ED 365 195. 64 pp. MF–01; PC not available EDRS.

Levinson, D.J., C.N. Darrow, E.B. Klein, M.A. Levinson, and B. McKee. 1978. *The Seasons of a Man's Life*. New York: Knopf.

Lloyd, S.R., and T. Berthelot. 1992. *Self-empowerment*. Los Altos, Calif.: Crisp Publications.

Long, J.S., and R. McGinnis. 1985. "The Effects of the Mentor on the Academic Career." *Scientometrics* 7(3–6): 255–80.

Luna, G. 1995. "Mentoring Experiences of Native American Faculty Members." Unpublished manuscript.

Luna, G., and D. Cullen. 1994a. "The Development of Female Leadership: Women Executives as Mentors." Paper presented at an annual meeting of the American Educational Research Association, April, New Orleans, Louisiana.

————. 1994b. "Executive Women: Experiences as Mentors and Protégés." *Central Business Review* 13(1): 21–25.

Maack, M.N., and J. Passet. 1994. *Aspirations and Mentoring in an Academic Environment: Women Faculty in Library and Information Science.* Westport, Conn.: Greenwood Press.

McNeer, E.J. 1983. "Two Opportunities for Mentoring: A Study of Women's Career Development in Higher Education Administration." *Journal of NAWDAC* 47(1): 8–14.

Madsen, M.K., and L.A. Blide. 1992. "Professional Advancement of Women in Health Care Management: A Conceptual Model." *Topics in Health Information Management* 13(2): 45–55.

Magner, D.K. 22 June 1994. "Academic Fields Where Women Predominate Pay Least, Survey Finds." *Chronicle of Higher Education* 40(42): A16.

————. 31 March 1995. "Tenure Reexamined." *Chronicle of Higher Education* 51(29): A17.

Martinko, M.J., and W.L. Gardner. 1982. "Learned Helplessness: An Alternative Explanation for Performance Deficits." *Academy of Management Review* 7: 195–205.

Menges, R.J., and W.H. Exum. 1983. "Barriers to the Progress of Women and Minority Faculty." *Journal of Higher Education* 54(2): 123–44.

Mertz, N., O. Welch, and J. Henderson. 1990. *Executive Mentoring: Myths, Issues, Strategies.* Newton, Mass.: WEEA Publishing Center.

Michael, J. 1992. "A Model of Managerial Networking Behavior." In *Proceedings from the Association of Management Conference,* Las Vegas, Nevada.

Mickelson, R.A., and M.L. Oliver. 1991. "Making the Short List: Black Candidates and the Faculty Recruitment Process." In *The Racial Crisis in American Higher Education,* edited by P.G. Altbach and K. Lomotey. Albany: State Univ. of New York Press.

Moore, K.M. 1982. "The Role of Mentors in Developing Leaders for Academe." *Educational Record* 63: 23–28.

Morrison, A.M., R.P. White, E. Van Velsor, and Center for Creative Leadership. 1992. *Breaking the Glass Ceiling: Can Women Reach the Top of America's Largest Corporations?* New York: Addison-Wesley.

Murray, M. 1991. *Beyond the Myths and Magic of Mentoring.* San Francisco: Jossey-Bass.

National Center for Education Statistics. 1994. *The Condition of Education, 1994.* NCES No. 94-149. Washington, D.C.: U.S.

Dept. of Education, Office of Educational Research and Improvement. ED 371 941. 475 pp. MF–01; PC–19.

National Commission on Working Women of Wider Opportunities for Women. Fall 1989. *Women and Nontraditional Work.* Washington, D.C.: American Federation of State, County, and Municipal Employees.

———. Winter 1990. *Women and Work.* Washington, D.C.: American Federation of State, County, and Municipal Employees.

National Education Association. 1991. "Minority Mentoring." In *Almanac of Higher Education.* Washington, D.C.: Author.

Nichols, I.A., H.M. Carter, and M.P. Golden. 1985. "The Patron System in Academia: Alternative Strategies for Empowering Academic Women." *Women's Studies International Forum* 8: 383–90.

Nieva, V.F., and B.A. Gutek. 1981. *Women and Work: A Psychological Perspective.* New York: Praeger.

Noe, R.A. 1988. "Women and Mentoring: A Review and Research Agenda." *Academy of Management Review* 13(1): 65–78.

Olian, J.D., S.J. Carroll, C.M. Giannantonia, and D.B. Feren. 1988. "What Do Protégés Look For in a Mentor? Results of Three Experimental Studies." *Journal of Vocational Behavior* 33: 15–37.

Padilla, A. 1994. "Ethnic Minority Scholars, Research, and Mentoring: Current and Future Issues." *Educational Researcher* 2(4): 24–27.

Parsons, M.H. 1992. "Quo Vadis: Staffing the People's College 2000." In *Maintaining Faculty Excellence,* edited by K. Kroll. New Directions for Community Colleges No. 37. San Francisco: Jossey-Bass.

Phillips, L.L. 1977. "Mentors and Protégés: A Study of the Career Development of Women Managers and Executives in Business and Industry." Ph.D. dissertation, Univ. of California, Los Angeles.

Phillips-Jones, L. 1982. *Mentors and Protégés.* New York: Arbor House.

———. 1983. "Establishing a Formalized Mentoring Program." *Training and Development Journal* 37: 38–42.

Queralt, M. 1982. "The Role of the Mentor in the Career Development of University Faculty." Paper presented at an annual conference of the National Association of Women Deans, Administrators, and Counselors. April, Indianapolis, Indiana. ED 216 614. 35 pp. MF–01; PC–02.

Ragins, B.R. 1989. "Barriers to Mentoring: The Female Manager's Dilemma." *Human Relations* 42(1): 1–22.

Rausch, D.K., B.P. Ortiz, R.A. Douthitt, and L.L. Reed. 1989. "The Academic Revolving Door: Why Do Women Get Caught?" *College and University Personnel Association Journal* 40: 1–16.

Reed, R.J. 1978. "Increasing the Opportunity for Black Students in Higher Education." *Journal of Negro Education* 47: 143–50.

Reich, M.H. 1986. "The Mentor Connection." *Personnel* 63(2): 50–56.

Reyes, M., and J.J. Halcon. 1991. "Practices of the Academy: Barriers to Access for Chicano Academics." In *The Racial Crisis in American Higher Education,* edited by P.G. Altbach and K. Lomotey. Albany: State Univ. of New York Press.

Riley, S., and D. Wrench. 1985. "Mentoring among Women Lawyers." *Journal of Applied Social Psychology* 15: 374–86.

Roche, G.R. 1979. "Probing: Much Ado about Mentors." *Harvard Business Review* 57: 14–16+.

Rosado, J. 1994. "Values and Conditions of Mentoring Latinos." In *Proceedings of the International Mentoring Association Annual Meeting, Diversity in Mentoring.* Kalamazoo: Western Michigan Univ.

Rosen, B., M. Miguel, and E. Peirce. 1989. "Stemming the Exodus of Women Managers." *Human Resource Management* 28: 475.

Rowan, R. 1994. "Comparing Teachers' Work with Work in Other Occupations: Notes on the Professional Status of Teaching." *Education Researcher* 23(6): 4–17.

Sandler, B.R. 10 March 1993. "Women as Mentors: Myths and Commandments." *Chronicle of Higher Education* 39(27): B3.

Sands, R.G., L.A. Parson, and J. Duane. 1991. "Faculty Mentoring Faculty at a Public University." *Journal of Higher Education* 62(2): 174–93.

———. 1992. "Faculty-Faculty Mentoring and Discrimination: Perceptions among Asian, Asian-American, and Pacific Island Faculty." *Equity and Excellence* 25(2–4): 124–29.

Schmidt, J.A., and J.S. Wolfe. 1980. "The Mentor Partnership: Discovery of Professionalism." *NASPA Journal* 17: 45–51.

Shakeshaft, C. 1987. *Women in Educational Administration.* Beverly Hills, Calif.: Sage.

Shandley, T.C. 1989. "The Use of Mentors for Leadership Development." *NASPA Journal* 27: 59–66.

Shea, C. 26 January 1994. "Women and Minorities Led the Way in a Year of Slow Enrollment Growth." *Chronicle of Higher Education* 50(20): A32.

Shoenfeld, A.C., and R. Magnan. 1992. *Mentor in a Manual.* Madison, Wisc.: Magna Publications.

Short, B., and M. Seeger. 1984. "Mentoring and Organizational Communication: A Review of the Research." Paper presented at an annual meeting of the Central States Speech Association, April, Chicago, Illinois. ED 245 282. 20 pp. MF–01; PC–01.

Sierra, C.M. 1993. "The University Setting Reinforces Inequality." In *Chicana Voices: Intersections of Class, Race, and Gender.* Albuquerque: Univ. of New Mexico Press, National Association for Chicano Studies.

Simeone, A. 1987. *Academic Women—Working towards Equality.* South Hadley, Mass.: Bergin & Garvey.

Solmon, L.C., and T.L. Wingard. 1991. "The Changing Demographics: Problems and Opportunities." In *The Racial Crisis in American Higher Education,* edited by P.G. Altbach and K. Lomotey. Albany: State Univ. of New York Press.

Stenberg, L. 1990. "Mentoring Home Economics Educators: Diversity or Homogeneity?" *Journal of Vocational Education Research* 15(1): 9–23.

Stewart, T.K. 1990. "Minority Excellence through Effective Mentoring." In *Mentoring Minorities and Women: A Challenge for Higher Education,* edited by A.D. Johnson and P. Mroczek. De Kalb: Northern Illinois Univ.

Strathan, A., L. Richardson, and J.A. Cook. 1991. *Gender and University Teaching: A Negotiated Difference.* New York: State Univ. of New York Press.

Swoboda, M.J., and S.B. Millar. 1986. "Networking-Mentoring: Career Strategy of Women in Academic Administration." *Journal of NAWDAC* 50(1): 8–13.

Takaki, R. 1989. *Strangers from a Different Shore: A History of Asian Americans.* New York: Penguin Books.

Talbert-Hersi, D. 1993. "A Comparison of Mentoring Need Differences between Black and White Faculty Women in Higher Education." Paper presented at the 6th Annual International Conference on Women in Higher Education, January, El Paso, Texas.

Tate, D.S., and C.L. Schwartz. Fall 1993. "Increasing the Retention of American Indian Students in Professional Programs in Higher Education." *Journal of American Indian Education* 33(1): 21–31.

Tracy, D. 1992. *Ten Steps to Empowerment.* New York: Quill.

U.S. Dept. of Labor. 1991. *Dictionary of Occupational Titles.* 4th ed. rev. Washington, D.C.: U.S. Government Printing Office.

Warihay, P.D. 1980. "The Climb to the Top: Is the Network the Route for Women?" *Personnel Administrator* 25(4): 55–60.

Warner, L.S. Spring 1992. "The Emergence of American Indian Higher Education." *Thought and Action* 8(1): 61–72.

Washington, E.M. 1989. "Western Michigan University's Black College Program: Selling the Black Faculty Cohort." In *Blacks in Higher Education: Overcoming the Odds,* edited by J. Elam. Lanham, Md.: University Press of America.

Wilson, J.A., and N.S. Elman. 1990. "Organizational Benefits of Mentoring." *Academy of Management Executive* 4(4): 88–94.

Wofford, M., A. Boysen, and L. Riding. September 1991. "A Research Mentoring Process." *ASHA:* 39–42.

Wright, C.A.. and S.D. Wright. 1987. "Young Professionals." *Family Relations* 36(2): 204–8.

Wunsch, M.A. 1993. "Mentoring Probationary Women Academics: A Pilot Programme for Career Development." *Studies in Higher Education* 18(3): 349–62.

Xu, M., and D. Newman. 1986. "Mentoring New Faculty in Higher Education Settings." Paper presented at an annual meeting of the American Evaluation Association, October 14–16. ED 293 428. 21 pp. MF–01; PC–01.

Yoder, J.D. 1985. "An Academic Woman as Token: A Case Study." *Journal of Social Issues* 41: 61–72.

Zey, M.G. 1984. *The Mentor Connection.* Homewood, Ill.: Dow Jones–Irwin.

———. 1986. "Only the Beginning: Five Major Trends that Signal the Growth of Corporate Formal Mentor Programs." *Proceedings of the First International Conference on Mentoring* 2: 147–52.

Zuckerman, H. 1970. "Stratification in American Science." In *Social Stratification,* edited by E.O. Laumann. Indianapolis: Bobbs-Merrill.

INDEX

A

Academic Council at Sinclair Community College, 68
Acceptance & Confirmation as a mentoring psychosocial function, 22
African-Americans
    1989 tenure rate of, 51
    faculty, 52–54
    most do not engage in mentoring in higher education, 53
    percentage of academic degrees conferred on, 47
Allocentrism as a basic cultural values of Hispanic faculty, 59
American Association for Higher Education
    project to reexamine the traditional processes of, 52
American Association of University Professors
    support for improving minority faculty participation, 47
American Indian
    1989 tenure rate of, 51
    percentage of academic degrees conferred of, 47
Any mentor and protégé can be paired is a mentoring myth, 62
Arizona Western College, Yuma faculty mentoring program, 75
Asian
    percentage of academic degrees conferred on, 47
    -American 1989 tenure rate of, 51
Asian faculty
    excluded from institutional support, 55
    have not adopted concept of mentoring, 55
    problems in academe, 54–55
Austin Community College, Texas faculty mentoring program, 75

B

Basic Trust versus Mistrust stage, 18
benefits of mentoring, 15

C

California State University, Los Angeles,
    faculty mentoring program at, 75
care, need for, 18
career
    advancement of junior employees linked to mentoring , 9
    development, 29–33
    functions of mentoring, 21, 22
    guide as a type of mentoring function, 31
Caretaker as basic building block
    for faculty and leadership development, 28
Caretaking as an operational limitations for women mentors, 43

Challenging Work as a mentoring career function, 22

childhood and adolescence as era of life cycle, 18

Coaching as a mentoring career function, 22

collegiality

    and consensus as a faculty promotion and tenure factor, 41

    as an important single factor in faculty development, 33

Collegial Peer function of, 23

Conceptualizing as basic building block

    for faculty and leadership development, 29

conflict of Generativity versus Stagnation stage, 18

Counseling as a mentoring psychosocial function, 22

cross-sex mentoring, 42–44

cultivation period of mentoring of Kram (1983), 20–21

custom and preference as a faculty promotion and tenure factor, 41

D

Dictionary of Occupational Titles (DOT), 5

E

early adulthood

    as era of life cycle, 18

    as novice phase, 19

Eastern Michigan University, Ypsilanti faculty mentoring program, 75

educational programs can increase understanding of mentoring, 3

empowering faculty, value of, 35

empowerment

    mentoring advances concept of individual and institutional, 1

    and Mentoring, 33–35

    by mentor, necessary components for, 34

    for others, ten principles for, 34–35

Enhancer as basic building block

    for faculty and leadership development, 28

Erikson Erik

    (1963), 4

    importance of mentoring in adult development, 37

    mentoring concepts of, 17

    stages of, 18

Exposure as a mentoring career function, 22

F

facilitated mentoring, definition of, 10

faculty and leadership development basic building blocks for,

    28–29

initiation period of mentoring of Kram (1983), 20
intellectual guide as a type of mentoring function, 31
invisible godparents, 10

K

K-12 setting advantages of mentoring in, 14
key principles for effective mentoring, 29–30
Kram (1983), 20-23
Kram (1986)
    characterized a hierarchy of mentoring functions, 17
    incremental hierarchical mentoring functions idea of, 28
Kram mentoring
    concepts of, 17
    definition centers around career and psychosocial function,
    21

L

late adulthood as era of life cycle, 18
Latino students
    description of, 57
    inequalities fostered by academic institutions, 58
lead ability as cause of achievement, 35
leadership mentor major responsibilities, 27–28
Levinson, Daniel
    mentoring concepts of, 17
    Seasons of, 18–20
Levinson, Darrow, Klein, Levinson, and McKee (1978), 4
    importance of mentoring in adult development, 37
life cycle
    overlapping eras of, 18
    theorists had powerful role models and mentors, 17
Los Medanos College, Pittsburg, California
    faculty mentoring program at, 75

M

McNeer (1983) research on difference in mentoring
    between educational and business organizations, 11
Madried, Arturo as former president of
    National Chicano Council on Higher Education, 58
Maintaining tradition as basic building block for faculty and
    leadership development, 29
Mentor
    as an exemplar, host and guide, sponsor and as a teacher, 4

as mentoring, 9

role models, behavior that often exhibit, 12

S

Same-Race Mentoring, value of, 59

same-sex mentoring, 42–44

secondary mentorship, 23

separation period of mentoring of Kram (1983), 21

"shadow organization" definition, 9

Shazam in Captain Marvel comics as mentor, 4

Simpatia as a basic cultural values of Hispanic faculty, 59

Sinclair Community College, 68

sink-or-swim approach, 32

socialization of faculty, mentoring in higher education defined as, 5

Socrates as mentor, 4

Southern Illinois University, Carbondale, Illinois
> faculty mentoring program at, 75

Special Peer function , 23

sponsor activities, 12

Sponsorship
> as a mentoring career functions, 22
> as a way of providing power to another, 35
> as interaction between junior and senior colleagues, 9

successful faculty mentoring guidelines and recommendations, 61

supportive bosses, 9

T

Teacher as building block for faculty and leadership development, 28

teaching as an obligation for female faculty in higher education, 41

The Odyssey, 3–4

The Seasons of a Man's Life (1978), 17

theories of Kram (1983), 20–23

Time
> as an operational limitations for women mentors, 43
> orientation as a basic cultural values of Hispanic faculty, 59

total quality management and quality assurance, 12

traditional mentors, 9

training necessary for mentors, 72

transmission of professional legacy by protégé empowerment, 34

U

University of

Albany, Albany, N. Y. faculty mentoring program at, 75

Alberta, Edmonton, Canada faculty mentoring program at, 75

Georgia, Athens, Georgia faculty mentoring program at, 75

V

virtues of mentoring, 63–64

W

Western Carolina University, Cullowhee, North Carolina

faculty mentoring at, 75

White percentage of academic degrees, 47

women

employees absence of mentors as major problem, 38

managers and executives mentors model of operational limitations for, 43 mentors teaching education, 41

Y

Yoda in *Star Wars* as mentor, 4

Z

Zazu in *The Lion King* as mentor, 4

ASHE-ERIC HIGHER EDUCATION REPORTS

Since 1983, the Association for the Study of Higher Education (ASHE) and the Educational Resources Information Center (ERIC) Clearinghouse on Higher Education, a sponsored project of the Graduate School of Education and Human Development at The George Washington University, have cosponsored the ASHE-ERIC Higher Education Report series. The 1995 series is the twenty-fourth overall and the seventh to be published by the Graduate School of Education and Human Development at The George Washington University.

Each monograph is the definitive analysis of a tough higher education problem, based on thorough research of pertinent literature and institutional experiences. Topics are identified by a national survey. Noted practitioners and scholars are then commissioned to write the reports, with experts providing critical reviews of each manuscript before publication.

Eight monographs (10 before 1985) in the ASHE-ERIC Higher Education Report series are published each year and are available on individual and subscription bases. To order, use the order form on the last page of this book.

Qualified persons interested in writing a monograph for the ASHE-ERIC Higher Education Report series are invited to submit a proposal to the National Advisory Board. As the preeminent literature review and issue analysis series in higher education, the Higher Education Reports are guaranteed wide dissemination and national exposure for accepted candidates. Execution of a monograph requires at least a minimal familiarity with the ERIC database, including *Resources in Education* and the *Current Index to Journals in Education*. The objective of these reports is to bridge conventional wisdom with practical research. Prospective authors are strongly encouraged to call Dr. Fife at 800-773-3742.

For further information, write to
    ASHE-ERIC Higher Education Reports
    The George Washington University
    One Dupont Circle, Suite 630
    Washington, DC 20036
Or phone (202) 296-2597; toll free: 800-773-ERIC.

Write or call for a complete catalog.

ADVISORY BOARD

James Earl Davis
University of Delaware at Newark

Susan Frost
Emory University

Mildred Garcia
Montclair State College

James Hearn
University of Georgia

Bruce Anthony Jones
University of Pittsburgh

L. Jackson Newell
Deep Springs College

Carolyn Thompson
State University of New York–Buffalo

G. Jeremiah Ryan
Harford Community College

Sherry Sayles-Folks
Eastern Michigan University

Karl Schilling
Miami University

Charles Schroeder
University of Missouri

Lawrence A. Sherr
University of Kansas

Patricia A. Spencer
Riverside Community College

Marilla D. Svinicki
University of Texas at Austin

David Sweet
OERI, U.S. Dept. of Education

Barbara E. Taylor
Association of Governing Boards

Donald H. Wulff
University of Washington

Manta Yorke
Liverpool John Moores University

REVIEW PANEL

Charles Adams
University of Massachusetts–Amherst

Louis Albert
American Association for Higher Education

Richard Alfred
University of Michigan

Henry Lee Allen
University of Rochester

Philip G. Altbach
Boston College

Marilyn J. Amey
University of Kansas

Kristine L. Anderson
Florida Atlantic University

Karen D. Arnold
Boston College

Robert J. Barak
Iowa State Board of Regents

Alan Bayer
Virginia Polytechnic Institute and State University

John P. Bean
Indiana University–Bloomington

John M. Braxton
Peabody College, Vanderbilt University

Ellen M. Brier
Tennessee State University

Barbara E. Brittingham
The University of Rhode Island

Dennis Brown
University of Kansas

Peter McE. Buchanan
Council for Advancement and Support of Education

Patricia Carter
University of Michigan

John A. Centra
Syracuse University

Arthur W. Chickering
George Mason University

Darrel A. Clowes
Virginia Polytechnic Institute and State University

Cynthia S. Dickens
Mississippi State University

Deborah M. DiCroce
Piedmont Virginia Community College

Sarah M. Dinham
University of Arizona

Kenneth A. Feldman
State University of New York–Stony Brook

Dorothy E. Finnegan
The College of William & Mary

Mildred Garcia
Montclair State College

Rodolfo Z. Garcia
Commission on Institutions of Higher Education

Kenneth C. Green
University of Southern California

James Hearn
University of Georgia

Edward R. Hines
Illinois State University

Deborah Hunter
University of Vermont

Philo Hutcheson
Georgia State University

Bruce Anthony Jones
University of Pittsburgh

Elizabeth A. Jones
The Pennsylvania State University

Kathryn Kretschmer
University of Kansas

Marsha V. Krotseng
State College and University Systems of West Virginia

George D. Kuh
Indiana University–Bloomington

Daniel T. Layzell
University of Wisconsin System

Patrick G. Love
Kent State University

Cheryl D. Lovell
State Higher Education Executive Officers

Meredith Jane Ludwig
American Association of State Colleges and Universities

Dewayne Matthews
Western Interstate Commission for Higher Education

Mantha V. Mehallis
Florida Atlantic University

Toby Milton
Essex Community College

James R. Mingle
State Higher Education Executive Officers

John A. Muffo
Virginia Polytechnic Institute and State University

L. Jackson Newell
Deep Springs College

James C. Palmer
Illinois State University

Robert A. Rhoads
The Pennsylvania State University

G. Jeremiah Ryan
Harford Community College

Mary Ann Danowitz Sagaria
The Ohio State University

Daryl G. Smith
The Claremont Graduate School

William G. Tierney
University of Southern California

Susan B. Twombly
University of Kansas

Robert A. Walhaus
University of Illinois–Chicago

Harold Wechsler
University of Rochester

Elizabeth J. Whitt
University of Illinois–Chicago

Michael J. Worth
The George Washington University

1995 ASHE-ERIC Higher Education Reports

1. Tenure, Promotion, and Reappointment: Legal and Administrative Implications
   Benjamin Baez and John A. Centra

2. Taking Teaching Seriously: Meeting the Challenge of Instructional Improvement
   Michael B. Paulsen and Kenneth A. Feldman

1994 ASHE-ERIC Higher Education Reports

1. The Advisory Committee Advantage: Creating an Effective Strategy for Programmatic Improvement
   Lee Teitel

2. Collaborative Peer Review: The Role of Faculty in Improving College Teaching
   Larry Keig and Michael D. Waggoner

3. Prices, Productivity, and Investment: Assessing Financial Strategies in Higher Education
   Edward P. St. John

4. The Development Officer in Higher Education: Toward an Understanding of the Role
   Michael J. Worth and James W. Asp II

5. The Promises and Pitfalls of Performance Indicators in Higher Education
   Gerald Gaither, Brian P. Nedwek, and John E. Neal

6. A New Alliance: Continuous Quality and Classroom Effectiveness
   Mimi Wolverton

7. Redesigning Higher Education: Producing Dramatic Gains in Student Learning
   Lion F. Gardiner

8. Student Learning outside the Classroom: Transcending Artificial Boundaries
   George D. Kuh, Katie Branch Douglas, Jon P. Lund, and Jackie Ramin-Gyurnek

1993 ASHE-ERIC Higher Education Reports

1. The Department Chair: New Roles, Responsibilities, and Challenges
   Alan T. Seagren, John W. Creswell, and Daniel W. Wheeler

2. Sexual Harassment in Higher Education: From Conflict to Community
   Robert O. Riggs, Patricia H. Marred, and JoAnn C. Cutting

3. Chicanos in Higher Education: Issues and Dilemmas for the 21st Century
   Adalberto Aguirre, Jr., and Ruben O. Martinez

4. Academic Freedom in American Higher Education: Rights, Responsibilities, and Limitations
   Robert K. Poch

5. Making Sense of the Dollars: The Costs and Uses of Faculty Compensation
   Kathryn M. Moore and Marilyn J. Amey

6. Enhancing Promotion, Tenure, and Beyond: Faculty Socialization as a Cultural Process
   William C. Tierney and Robert A. Rhoads

7. New Perspectives for Student Affairs Professionals: Evolving Realities, Responsibilities, and Roles
   Peter H. Garland and Thomas W. Grace

8. Turning Teaching into Learning: The Role of Student Responsibility in the Collegiate Experience
   Todd M. Davis and Patricia Hillman Murrell

1992 ASHE-ERIC Higher Education Reports

1. The Leadership Compass: Values and Ethics in Higher Education
   John R. Wilcox and Susan L. Ebbs

2. Preparing for a Global Community: Achieving an International Perspective in Higher Education
   Sarah M. Pickert

3. Quality: Transforming Postsecondary Education
   Ellen Earle Chaffee and Lawrence A. Sherr

4. Faculty Job Satisfaction: Women and Minorities in Peril
   Martha Wingard Tack and Carol Logan Patitu

5. Reconciling Rights and Responsibilities of Colleges and Students: Offensive Speech, Assembly, Drug Testing, and Safety
   Annette Gibbs

6. Creating Distinctiveness: Lessons from Uncommon Colleges and Universities
   Barbara K. Townsend, L. Jackson Newell, and Michael D. Wiese

7. Instituting Enduring Innovations: Achieving Continuity of Change in Higher Education
   Barbara K. Curry

8. Crossing Pedagogical Oceans: International Teaching Assistants in U.S. Undergraduate Education
   Rosslyn M. Smith, Patricia Byrd, Gayle L. Nelson, Ralph Pat Barrett, and Janet C. Constantinides

1991 ASHE-ERIC Higher Education Reports

1. Active Learning: Creating Excitement in the Classroom
   Charles C. Bonwell and James A. Eison

2. Realizing Gender Equality in Higher Education: The Need to Integrate Work/Family Issues
   Nancy Hensel

3. Academic Advising for Student Success: A System of Shared Responsibility
   Susan H. Frost

4. Cooperative Learning: Increasing College Faculty Instructional Productivity
   David W. Johnson, Roger T. Johnson, and Karl A. Smith

5. High School–College Partnerships: Conceptual Models, Programs, and Issues
   Arthur Richard Greenberg

6. Meeting the Mandate: Renewing the College and Departmental Curriculum
   William Toombs and William Tierney

7. Faculty Collaboration: Enhancing the Quality of Scholarship and Teaching
   Ann E. Austin and Roger G. Baldwin

8. Strategies and Consequences: Managing the Costs in Higher Education
   John S. Waggaman

1990 ASHE-ERIC Higher Education Reports

1. The Campus Green: Fund Raising in Higher Education
   Barbara E. Brittingham and Thomas R. Pezzullo

2. The Emeritus Professor: Old Rank, New Meaning
   James E. Mauch, Jack W. Birch, and Jack Matthews

3. "High-Risk" Students in Higher Education: Future Trends
   Dionne J. Jones and Betty Collier Watson

4. Budgeting for Higher Education at the State Level: Enigma, Paradox, and Ritual
   Daniel T. Layzell and Jan W. Lyddon

5. Proprietary Schools: Programs, Policies, and Prospects
   John B. Lee and Jamie P. Merisotis

6. College Choice: Understanding Student Enrollment Behavior
   Michael B. Paulsen

7. Pursuing Diversity: Recruiting College Minority Students
   Barbara Astone and Elsa Nuñez-Wormack

8. Social Consciousness and Career Awareness: Emerging Link in Higher Education
   John S. Swift Jr.

1989 ASHE-ERIC Higher Education Reports

1. Making Sense of Administrative Leadership: The 'L' Word in Higher Education
   Estela M. Bensimon, Anna Neumann, and Robert Birnbaum

2. Affirmative Rhetoric, Negative Action: African-American and Hispanic Faculty at Predominantly White Universities
   Valora Washington and William Harvey

3. Postsecondary Developmental Programs: A Traditional Agenda with New Imperatives
   Louise M. Tomlinson

4. The Old College Try: Balancing Athletics and Academics in Higher Education
   John R. Thelin and Lawrence L. Wiseman

5. The Challenge of Diversity: Involvement or Alienation in the Academy?
   Daryl G. Smith

6. Student Goals for College and Courses: A Missing Link in Assessing and Improving Academic Achievement
   Joan S. Stark, Kathleen M. Shaw, and Malcolm A. Lowther

7. The Student as Commuter: Developing a Comprehensive Institutional Response
   Barbara Jacoby

8. Renewing Civic Capacity: Preparing College Students for Service and Citizenship
   Suzanne W. Morse

ORDER FORM

Quantity   **Amount**

_____ Please begin my subscription to the 1995 *ASHE-ERIC Higher Education Reports* at $98.00, 31% off the cover price, starting with Report 1, 1995. Includes shipping. _____

_____ Please send a complete set of the 1994 *ASHE-ERIC Higher Education Reports* at $98.00, 31% off the cover price. Please add shipping charge below. _____

Individual reports are available at the following prices:
1993, 1994, and 1995, $18.00; 1988–1992, $17.00; 1980–1987, $15.00

SHIPPING CHARGES
For orders of more than 50 books, please call for shipping information.

	1st three books	*Ea. addl. book*
U.S., 48 Contiguous States		
Ground:	$3.75	$0.15
2nd Day*:	8.25	1.10
Next Day*:	18.00	1.60
Alaska & Hawaii (2nd Day Only)*:	13.25	1.40

U.S. Territories and Foreign Countries: Please call for shipping information.
*Order will be shipped within 24 hours of request.
All prices shown on this form are subject to change.

PLEASE SEND ME THE FOLLOWING REPORTS:

Quantity	Report No.	Year	Title	Amount

Please check one of the following:

☐ Check enclosed, payable to GWU-ERIC.
☐ Purchase order attached ($45.00 minimum).
☐ Charge my credit card indicated below:
    ☐ Visa   ☐ MasterCard

Expiration Date_____

Subtotal: _____
Shipping: _____
Total Due: _____

Name_____

Title_____

Institution _____

Address_____

City _____ State _____ Zip_____

Phone _____ Fax _____Telex_____

Signature _____ Date_____

SEND ALL ORDERS TO: ASHE-ERIC Higher Education Reports
                      The George Washington University
                      One Dupont Cir., Ste. 630, Washington, DC 20036-1183
                      Phone: (202) 296-2597 • Toll-free: 800-773-ERIC